PRAISE FOR THE VELOURS

There are many groups who have contributed a song to the 500 or so that comprise my Top 10. The Velours have given me two. I'm still as crazy over "Can I Come Over Tonight" and "Remember" as I was back in the 50s.

- Marv Goldberg,
  Writer & Music Historian

KEEPING DOO-WOP ALIVE

One Man's Story of Strength, Stamina & Survival as an International Entertainer

KEEPING DOO-WOP ALIVE

One Man's Story of Strength, Stamina & Survival as an International Entertainer

JOHN CHEATDOM

WITH

YVONNE ROSE

FALSETTO PRESS

London, England

KEEPING DOO-WOP ALIVE

Published by: Falsetto Press
London, England
jtcheatdom@hotmail.com

John Cheatdom, Publisher / Editorial Director
Quality Press.info, Book Packager

Paperback ISBN #: 978-1-937269-82-1
Ebook ISBN #: 978-1-937269-83-8
Library of Congress Control Number: 2018937294

DEDICATION

Many people have been instrumental to my Career Advancement and left an unforgettable imprint in my life. For those who have earned their angel wings, R.I.P. and for those who continue to enrich my journey through your words and deeds, God bless you. From the bottom of my heart, I dedicate "Keeping Doo Wop Alive" to each and every one of you:

Donald Haywoode, who was so instrumental to my career – as a friend and Musical Guru.

Richard Barret "Mr Doo Wop" was responsible for the success of many groups in the 50s & 60s.

Peter Stringfellow initiated the transformation from "The Velours" to "The Fantastics" in England.

Sgig Gene Washington, deputy for the Orient & Western Europe, my childhood friend who guided me to reach great heights in Masonry.

Heiko Gunter, Germany, my trusted agent for over 20 years,

Mr. (Doctor) M, Keene, Throat Surgeon at St Bartholomew Hospital, London whose delicate hands saved my singing career.

The team of doctors in the Rheumatology clinic of The Homerton University college, London, who have helped me in my battle with painful crippling Rheumatoid arthritis over the years.

Reverend Lou Phillips, Washington DC., who gave me the inspiration to write this book.

Cliff Dunbar, London, my close friend and Hairdresser for over 30 years, "He's kept me pretty!" Check out the styles in the *Generation* DVD.

Ricky Daniel London, my long-time Business Adviser.

Andrew Thompson - Lee & Thompson Solicitors of London. One of the nicest persons I've ever met and a truly great music lawyer.

ACKNOWLEDGEMENTS

I was lucky to be part of a music generation that produced some of the greatest musical icons ever to grace a stage. *An Icon is an artist whose body oozes with stardust, we call them "SANGERS".*

Working with these great performers only made me a better performer and their lasting friendships in addition to the support they gave me, especially in my younger days, is for me… ***totally unforgettable***.

This book is in their honour.

1. Ms Judy Cheeks.
2. Cathy Sledge – SISTER SLEDGE.
3. Valerie Holiday – THREE DEGREES.
4. Arlene Smith, Jackie Landry, Lois Harris, Renee Minus and Sonia Goring – THE CHANTELS.
5. Earnestine and Shirley Pearce, Viola Billups – THE FLIRTATIONS.
6. Gladys and Bubba Knight, Edward Patten and William Guest – THE PIPS.
7. Liz and Thomas Pemberton – BONY M.
8. Chuck Willis. (The God-Father of my soul)
9. Billy Henderson – The SPINNERS.
10. Otis Williams – THE TEMPTATIONS.
11. Nate Nelson – THE FLAMINGOS.
12. George Chandler – FOUR KENTS and LONDON BEAT.

13. George Williams – The TYMES.
14. Sammy Strain – THE CHIPS, LITTLE ANTHONY and THE IMPERIALS, THE O'JAYS.
15. Clem Curtis – The FOUNDATIONS.
16. Johnny Moore, Bill Fredericks – THE DRIFTERS.
17. Anthony Gordine, Clarence Collins, Ernest Wright and Kenny Seymour – LITTLE ANTHONY AND THE IMPERIALS.
18. Marvin Junior, Chuck Barksdale, Mickey McGill, Johnny Funghess, Johnny Carter – THE DELLS.
19. Eugene Record, Marshall Thompson Robert Lester – THE CHI – LITES.
20. Edwin Starr – (The king of them all)
21. Butch and Chubby Tavares.
22. Gary Gant, Bob Rivers, Billy Morris and Herman Cofield – THE INVITATIONS.

CONTENTS

FOREWORD

There are many stories to be told about many great artists in the music business. ***Keeping Doo-Wop Alive*** tells the story of another one. It is the story of singer, John Cheatdom, who started his professional entertainment career in 1957, at the age of 17, and is still working to the present day.

It is the story of what it is like to be a member of a vocal group. Not as easy a job as you might think. It speaks of the ups and downs and the changing phases of the music industry over more than 60 years.

After starting his recording career as a member of The Velours and making a life-changing move to England in 1967, John had success with The Fantastics, The Realistics, and The Magic Platters.

Keeping Doo-Wop Alive is a wonderful read for anybody interested in the world of black vocal group music by a man who has seen it all.

George Chandler

July 4, 2017

PREFACE

The expression "what comes up must come down", clearly describes my chosen profession of the last 60 years, Show business or the music business.

<u>The upside:</u>

Hit records, fame, touring, money, women and the world at your feet.

<u>The downside:</u>

Being ripped off by unscrupulous managers, agents and accountants - who you have trusted with your life, bankruptcy, broken homes and watching group members destroy themselves through alcohol and drugs… and finally back to your 9 to 5.

I have been on this merry-go-round four times over the years with four different successful singing groups: The Velours, The Fantastics, The Realistics and The Magic Platters. Each time, I dust myself off and start again with a new challenge and a goal of ***Keeping Doo-Wop Alive***.

I am truly blessed to be a part of the history of Doo-Wop, a genre of music that was developed in African American communities - New York, Philadelphia, Chicago, Baltimore, Washington, Pittsburgh, Cincinnati, Detroit and Los Angeles in the 1940s, achieving mainstream popularity in the 1950s and early 1960s. During those early years, all the group singers knew each other and would not hesitate to gather in a club or on a street corner, just to sing harmony.

Built upon vocal harmony, doo-wop was one of the most mainstream, pop-oriented R&B styles of the time, which featured a high tenor singing the lead and a bass singer reciting the lyrics in the middle of the song. Doo-Wop features vocal group harmony, nonsense syllables, a simple beat, sometimes little or no instrumentation, and simple music and lyrics, which are usually about a boy and a girl and the love they found and lost.

As a first tenor, I fit right into the Doo-Wop era and never had a problem finding my niche, always on top of the harmony, they called me the glue.

By the end of the 50s the Doo-Wop style was phased out and put under the umbrella of rock and roll, but its spirit can still be heard in the music of today. ***Doo-Wop will never die.***

INTRODUCTION

I always had a passion for music. It was in my genes. My mother's mother - my grandmother - was the child of second generation slaves. She was born into slavery and raised in a close-knit environment where, as often as they could, the elders sang and chanted the old African songs. Singing kept the slaves connected to their roots in Africa, but it also calmed their souls, gave them hope and kept them alive. My grandmother always sang to my mother and so on down the line.

My mother, Kathleen Cheatdom, was a child protégé, a gifted musician who earned college scholarships by singing and playing the piano. We didn't talk much about her dreams; but I imagine she would have loved to have a musical career, had it not been for her early gift of motherhood, which set her on a different path.

The musical gifts my mother inherited were passed down to me. I grew up listening to her play the piano; and then to earn extra income, she used to give piano lessons to children in the neighbourhood. When I turned five-years-old, my mother wanted to teach me, too. Oftentimes, when I was outside playing ball with my friends, she told me it was time to take my piano lessons. So, reluctantly, I would have to go in the house and there were usually two or three girls in there taking lessons from her. I wanted to get back to the ballgame, but my mother had a ruler that she used to hit me with if I didn't cooperate. So, I had to sit and wait for my lessons, until the girls had finished.

We had a "player piano" - one of those self-playing pianos with the music roller inside. A mechanism operated the piano action via pre-programmed music recorded on perforated paper. If you hit a chord it would play music, almost like a record player. My mother used to get all the songs that were published at the time, which were placed on the music roll and then put inside the piano. We would play and the piano notes would move… that's how she used to teach us to play specific songs.

Sales for the player piano peaked in 1924, then declined as the improvement in phonograph recordings (records) developed in the mid-1920s. The advent of electrical amplification in home music reproduction via radio in the same period helped cause their eventual decline in popularity of the player piano, and the stock market crash of 1929 virtually wiped out production.

One of my mother's students was a Mexican girl named Florene Brezel. She became a classical star because of my mother's lessons – I'll never forget her.

As a child, unlike my mother, the piano did not excite me very much; but I loved hearing the songs on the piano and I loved to sing. I always sang in church and in school choirs. When I connected with friends who had similar passions for music I evolved, joined a group and became a professional entertainer. I have done nothing else my entire life…just singing. I consider myself truly blessed and I still feel the rhythms and beats from my ancestors' drums and chants.

My mother and I attended one of the largest churches in Brooklyn - First AME Zion, which had three choirs. We had the adult choir, the intermediate choir and the senior choir. Ordinarily, I would have been in the intermediate choir, but I used to sing higher than the girls so they put me in the senior choir, which was very unusual.

After being raised with strong ties to the church and after sharing my vocal talents with the church congregation for many years, I am sure my mother was extremely disappointed when I announced that I wasn't going to sing in the choir anymore.

My mother was one if the trustees at the church; but she never did anything musical there… she didn't want to play piano in the church. I am not sure if they even knew she had any musical talent. All she wanted to do was be a trustee in church and teach piano to the neighbourhood girls. Since she was giving piano lessons, as well as working a full-time job, she didn't have a lot of spare time to attend choir rehearsals. And I guess she figured that since I was representing the Cheatdom family in the choir, there was no need for her to offer her musical talents there, as well.

From the time I was around nine-years-old, until my voice changed I used to earn a lot of money at church. As we all know, in most churches in America, the biggest crowds you're going to get are on Easter and Mother's Day. The First AME Zion had more than 1000 people in attendance on those days. Whenever I stood up to sing solos they would pass a briefcase around and I would earn at least $500 to $600 in just one day.

It was good while it lasted, but when I got to be about eleven-years-old, my voice started changing and I told my mother, "Now I've got to stop singing with this choir." My mother counted on my earnings from those special church concerts, so she asked me, "Can you do one more year?" Reluctantly, I granted her request, but shortly thereafter, as soon as I turned twelve-years-old, I left the choir.

I had made up my mind to quit singing in the choir and my mother couldn't persuade me to continue. I fervently believe that I would not have the successful music career that propelled me through life without the foundation of the church choir. It was good training and a great experience, while it lasted. Word got out about my "beautiful voice" and I was becoming a mini-star in Brooklyn. When I used to sit up there with the choir, I couldn't wait for the preacher to finish his sermon because the people in the congregation always wanted me to sing solo. *It was the funniest thing*...and it was financially rewarding as well. Can you imagine being a young boy, at the age of ten, making $500 in one day by doing what he loved - singing?

Once I started singing with the Troubadours, I didn't go back to the church anymore. That drove a little wedge between my mother and me, but eventually, we bonded on a different level. I refer to the experience as my "Coming of Age." My mother never said she was proud of me or my choice, but I always felt her pride whenever she would see me perform or talk to her friends about me.

Speaking of church, we had an interesting experience when we started singing professionally. One of the guys in the group was Catholic. *Now imagine being Catholic back in the early 50s.* We were touring down south in Georgia and he said, “Can you guys come to church service with me? I am Catholic and I want to attend a Catholic church.” So, we decided to go with him to the church, but the ushers wouldn’t let us enter. So, I asked him “Why do you want to be a Catholic if you can’t even go into the church?”

The racism we experienced in the Catholic church was totally shocking and I remember thinking, *Well, maybe it will be different once we get out of the South.* Then later, when we were in Flint, Michigan we went up the steps that led to a big Catholic cathedral; but, again, one of the ushers stopped us at the door and said, “Do you want to come in?” We replied, “Yes.” Then he told us we could come in, but we would have to stand in the back of the church. It was a massive sanctuary and there were plenty of seats available. I couldn’t believe that we were directed to *stand in the back*, and this was up north, in Michigan. It was a terrible experience. That’s when the realization hit me - racism was not just a “southern” thing.

When I became a “grown man,” every bit of eighteen-years-old, I was on the road with many great blues and R & B legends touring the country, and eventually, the world. We had countless experiences -

adventures, mentors, influences – and we crossed paths with a variety of people of many faiths, religions and nationalities.

My hope is that everyone who has a passion for music, who reads about or hears about my story, will become inspired to follow in my footsteps. And, no matter what it takes to embark upon your journey and how it evolves, I hope you can become disciplined and dedicated enough to live your dream, too.

ONE

MY NAME IS JOHN CHEATDOM

I was born in Brooklyn, New York, July 7, 1938, where my mother, Mrs. Kathleen Cheatdom raised me until I turned fifteen. I guess you might say, at that point, I took over the helm and raised myself into manhood.

My name is John Cheatdom. I am probably the only living singer who has had success in five different singing groups – The Troubadors, The Velours, The Fantastics, The Realistics and The Magic Platters. I have spent close to 70 years of my life performing throughout the world, in five different continents.

My professional music career began in 1953 when our group was originally formed as The Troubadours in the Bedford-Stuyvesant area of Brooklyn.

Bedford–Stuyvesant also known as "Bed–Stuy" is a neighbourhood of 153,000 inhabitants in the north central portion of the New York City borough of Brooklyn.

For decades, "Bed-Stuy" has been a cultural center for Brooklyn's African American population. Following the construction of the IND Fulton Street Line in 1936, African Americans left an overcrowded Harlem for greater housing availability in Bedford–Stuyvesant. From there, African Americans have since moved into the surrounding areas of Brooklyn, such as East New York, Crown Heights, Brownsville, and Fort Greene. Bedford–Stuyvesant has many historic brownstones.

The original members of The Troubadours were Jerome "Romeo" Ramos (tenor; May 15, 1937 – October 21, 2012), Marvin Holland (bass), Sammy Gardner (lead) and me – I sang tenor. In 1955, Gardner left to join the army and was replaced by my cousin, Kenneth Walker. We were considered a doo-wop group and we performed locally. On one occasion, The Troubadours performed at the Apollo Amateur Hour, in Harlem, where we opened for Nat King Cole.

The Troubadours had little success, until in 1956, we added a fifth singer, tenor Donald Haywoode (August 24, 1936 – August 9, 2015). We wanted a name that would sound more sophisticated; so, when Donald joined the group, we changed the name to The Velours. We made our first recordings for the Onyx label, before Marvin and Kenneth left the group and were replaced by John Pearson and Charles Moffitt (September 6, 1929 – December 1986). Then we also added a pianist, Calvin McClean.

During the next two years, The Velours made some of our best-remembered records for Onyx, including "Can I Come Over Tonight" written by Donald Haywoode. The song reached number 83 on the *Billboard* pop chart in 1957. I was nineteen-years-old at the time. We had further chart success the following year with "Remember", with Jerome Ramos as lead vocalist. “Remember” also reached number 83 on the *Billboard* pop chart. Years later, the group later recorded an LP, *Remember with the Velours*. We regularly performed at the Apollo Theatre, and shared stages with such stars as Roy Brown, Fats Domino, Larry Williams and Bo Diddley.

After adding a sixth singer, Troy Keyes, we recorded for several small New York labels through the late 1950s and early 1960s, including George Goldner's Gone Records, but with little success. *George Goldner (February 9, 1918 – April 15, 1970) was an American record label owner, record producer and promoter who played an important role in establishing the popularity of rock and roll in the 1950s, by recording and promoting many groups and records that appealed to young people across racial boundaries. Among the acts he discovered were the Crows, Frankie Lymon and the Teenagers, and Little Anthony and the Imperials.*

TWO

FROM WHENCE I CAME

My mother Kathleen Anderson was born in Bluefield in Gary, West Virginia in 1906. My maternal grandmother's name was Mollie Anderson and my grandfather's name was Lawrence William Anderson.

Mollie was raised on a plantation in West Virginia and, as fate would have it, met and married Lawrence, the love of her life, nearby in her home state. He worked in the coal mines, she was a housewife. Because there were no records made at the time of Mollie's birth, she didn't know how old she was; but because of certain events that she described to the family, they estimated her year of birth to be around1885. My grandmother died in 1977 at the approximate age of 92.

My grandparents were wonderful. They looked after me often when I was a baby and so did my mother's brothers. The family was very influential and full of great role models. My grandfather's sister, Elizabeth, was a professor at Virginia Theological Seminary and College. The school's library was dedicated to her. My great Aunt Elizabeth's husband, William Cooper, was head of the Barber College on campus in Petersburg, Virginia.

As a young child, I lived in New York, but my mother often took me to visit my grandparents. Every summer, in June, when I finished school in New York, I would go down South and spend the summer in Gary with my cousins. My classes at home didn't resume until early September, right after Labor Day. However, my southern cousins used to go back to school in August, so their teachers would allow me to go to school with them for two weeks. I would sit in their classes and I was totally amazed at things that they used to learn – particularly, Black History.

When I went back to school in Brooklyn, I would tell my friends, "Hey, you know, I learned something interesting!" They would not believe me when I told them about the accomplishments of so many African Americans, who went un-noted in the northern states. My friends told me, "Get out of here, John! Black people ain't done nothing, man. Get out of here!" So, I said, "I'm serious, man. I got the book!" Then they would tell me, "Come on man, get out of here. That can't be true! We never learn any stuff like that in school in New York about Black people in America!"

Living in New York was such a different lifestyle from living in the south. Although there was segregation down south, it had such a distinctive, more positive vibe than that in the north. Even as a young boy, the things I learned at the southern schools about African Americans, as a people, filled me with pride about my heritage. It sparked a togetherness that I had never felt in New York. My family was very close-knit and I just loved it. I asked my mother if I could stay in West Virginia and go to school there, year-round; but she wouldn't allow me to do that. She said, "No, you've got to go to school in New York." So, I reluctantly went back to New York, and that's where I was when the music won me over.

My mother had two brothers - Uncle Tommy and Uncle Jimmy, and a sister -Aunt Kacey. Aunt Kacey was a housewife and her husband was a coal miner. Uncle Tommy also worked at the coal mines, but Uncle Jimmy was an undertaker. Both my uncles played basketball, really well. Uncle Tommy and Aunt Kacey were dark-skinned; but my mother and Uncle Jimmy were light-skinned. My mother would tell me stories about how she and her siblings used to fight each other all the time - the darks against the lights. *Some things have never changed.*

My grandparents and my Uncle Jimmy remained in the South. Later, after I moved to England, I used to go back to West Virginia, as often as possible; just to see my grandparents and to spend some quality time with them. We loved each other very much.

My Uncle Jimmy was a pretty boy. He was tall and good looking. *People used to say I took after him in the looks' department*. Because he was a very skilled undertaker, when miners used to get injured or killed in the mines, he would go there to help them and their families by using his reconstructive skills on the unfortunate victims. Sometimes he would even have to rebuild the non-surviving victims' faces. Other undertakers used to call Uncle Jimmy for all the real difficult jobs that they would have to deal with back in those days. He was so talented to the point that he would get job offers from large establishments that tried to get him to move to New York to work for them as an undertaker. But, Uncle Jimmy loved his job down South and he wouldn't consider relocating, so he just stayed in West Virginia where he worked as an undertaker until he died.

Uncle Tommy and his wife, Lee, had two children - Phyllis and Larry. When the coal mines closed, their family moved to Washington D.C. where Uncle Tommy got a job working for the government and Aunt Lee became a housewife. They were wonderful people, I was very fond of them.

We were a very close-knit family. My two cousins were like my brother and sister. They were younger than me, but because I was an only child, we spent a lot of time together. It was always the three of us - Phyllis, Larry and me. Later, when the Velours used to go to Washington, D.C. to perform at the Howard Theatre, I would bring Phyllis and Larry backstage to meet all the stars. They loved that and would always say, "My cousin's a star! My cousin John is a star." Those were really wonderful times that have left me with great memories.

My aunts, uncles and first cousins on the Anderson side of the family have all passed away. But, their children and grandchildren – my second and third cousins - continue to add branches to the Anderson family tree. Uncle Tommy, his wife and children all passed away within a five-year cycle of each other. In 2015, my cousin Larry died suddenly from a blood clot in his leg. His sister Phyllis died a year before Larry in 2014; she had heart attack. Uncle Tommy's wife, Aunt Lee also died in 2014 and Uncle Tommy died three years prior to Aunt Lee in 2011.

My mother lived a long and productive life, she died in the year 2000, at the age of 94. I was on tour in Argentina, at the time; so, I flew from Argentina and my wife, Rona, flew from London to New York along with my two youngest sons, Jamie and Blake, to attend the funeral.

THREE

WHERE IT ALL BEGAN

My mother, Kathleen Anderson Cheatdom was the biggest influence in my music career. Back in the 1920s, when Kathleen was a child, the United States was segregated. She attended Gary High School, which was the "coloured" school, at that time. Kathleen was a gifted classical pianist, one of the first young "colored" concert pianists in the United States. The petite young lady was a "girl wonder" and the talk of the town. At only 5 feet tall, she had to sit on pillows to reach the keyboard and her feet barely touched the pedals. After Kathleen graduated from Gary High, she received several scholarships and went to three different colleges: Bluefield College, Morgan College and Virginia Theological Seminary and College. Unfortunately, she never graduated from any of them.

In 1922, Bluefield College opened its doors to students seeking Christian higher education in Southwestern Virginia. Morgan State University (commonly referred to as MSU, Morgan State, or Morgan) is a public research university and historically black college (HBCU) located in Baltimore, Maryland, United States. Morgan is Maryland's designated public urban university and the largest HBCU in Maryland. In 1890 the university, formerly known as the "Centenary Biblical

Institute," changed its name to Morgan College to honor Reverend Lyttleton Morgan. It became a "university" in 1975. In 1886, the Virginia Baptist State Convention founded the Lynchburg Baptist Seminary as an institution of "self-reliance," "racial pride," and "faith." It first offered classes in 1890 as the renamed Virginia Seminary. Under the direction of Gregory Willis Hayes, the second president of the college, who served from 1891 to 1906, the school became a pioneer in the field of African American Education. In 1900, the school was reincorporated as the Virginia Theological Seminary and College, and in 1962, it became the Virginia Seminary and College. The college was renamed and incorporated as Virginia University of Lynchburg in 1996.

Kathleen was a bit of a play-girl and she used to have a lot of fun. The universities didn't take too kindly to her partying antics, so after she would get a scholarship they would cancel it. But at the time, because she was such a sought-after pianist, she had no problem moving on to another college.

That's how my mother met my father, John Cheatdom, who was a college professor at Morgan College. She caught his eye one night at a social gathering, while they were both, coincidentally, enjoying the same drink – bourbon and ginger on the rocks. Soon after they met, John and Kathleen started dating, fell in love, and got married. Unfortunately, my parent's marriage was short-lived. I am a product of their marriage, but I never knew my father because he died from pneumonia six months before I was born. Later in life, I tried to locate my father's family – the Cheatdoms – but I never could find any of them.

John and Kathleen were living in West Virginia when they met and married. After my father died, my mother was heartbroken. At the age of 32, Kathleen left West Virginia with my Aunt Algie, who was my grandfather's youngest sister. *She and my mother were around the same age*. They went up north to New York to look for work and three months later, I was born.

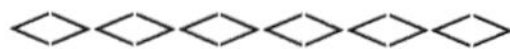

Shortly thereafter, Aunt Algie met the man who would later become her husband and my uncle, Mr. John Peach, a longshoreman. Uncle John was big-boned and about six-feet-two inches tall. His father was Irish, his mother was black; and Uncle John looked like John Wayne. He had a motorcycle. When I was just six-years-old, he used to put me on the back of it, go down to the bar and "work out." John Peach would enter the bar and the next thing you knew he was involved in a big fight. He would sit me on the bar stool, knock out a couple of guys, and then drink some whiskey. After he finished drinking, Uncle John would put me back on the motorcycle and take me home. I loved and admired my uncle, he was an amazing guy. He's the closest person that I'd ever known as a father.

FOUR

REMEMBERING "RED HOOK"

Aunt Algie, Uncle John, my mother and I all lived together in downtown South Brooklyn, also known as Red Hook, on Warren Street. Back in those days, downtown Brooklyn, down by the docks was known as the "dark city."

Red Hook had a reputation as the toughest section of Brooklyn. Al Capone got his start as a small-time criminal there, along with his wound that led to his nickname, "Scarface." In 1950, at the peak of the era of longshoremen, 21,000 people, with more than a third of them under the age of 18, lived in the neighbourhood. Many of the people lived in the Red Hook Houses, which were among the first and largest Federal Housing projects in the country. The Red Hook Houses were row houses, built the year I was born, in 1938, for families of dockworkers. My family lived in an apartment building right around the corner from them.

Eventually, two major events would influence Red Hook's fate: the 1946 opening of the Gowanus Expressway and the 1950 opening of the Brooklyn Battery Tunnel cut off the neighbourhood from the rest of the borough. So, in 1944 when the reconstruction was in its planning stages, Aunt Algie, Uncle John, my mother and I left Warren Street and relocated a little further up into the middle of Brooklyn, to Dean Street. We continued to live together on Dean Street until my mother met and married my Boy Scout leader, William Adams.

I still have fond memories of my youth. But after the peak of the 1950s, Red Hook suffered a loss of jobs, population and geographical isolation. Over the next decade or so, the neighbourhood bled jobs, as shipping underwent a dramatic change. Manufacturing fell by one-half, and the Brooklyn dockyards were largely abandoned. Uncle John had to seek other employment before the Brooklyn Navy Yard closed in 1966.

Today, much of Red Hook's waterfront has become park-land and retail. The neighbourhood continues to draw the curious from outside, along with a trickle of tourists, the residents of the Red Hook Houses, and a swell of activists and artists who are tempted by the low rents, industrial aspects, old world charm, and astounding views. Although the history of my old neighbourhood is also intertwined with the ill-conceived plans of state and city government, I must admit, it has undergone a beautiful transition.

I don't go back to New York often, but whenever I do, I always make it a point to visit my childhood "home town" of Bed-Stuy.

FIVE

MOVING ON UP

Dean Street, my second home in Brooklyn, was a melting pot, just like Red Hook had been. It was a culturally-mixed community. There were two buildings that housed "colored" people and, back then, that included the Puerto Ricans. There were also a lot of Irish, some Jews and a few Chinese in the community, but everybody got along fine.

At that time, the Brooklyn Dodgers' baseball team was the main talking-point, because there was no NFL or NBA. It was just "baseball and The Brooklyn Dodgers," who we all idolized. The Brooklyn Dodgers' team is noted for signing Jackie Robinson in 1947 as the first "colored" player in the modern major leagues. The Brooklyn Dodgers were active in the major leagues from 1884 until 1957, after which the team moved to Los Angeles, where it continued its history as the "Los Angeles Dodgers". The team's name was derived from the reputed skill of Brooklyn residents at evading (dodging) the city's trolley streetcar network.

When I started going to PS 9 Junior High, I would ride the famous trolley streetcar to school. Eventually the trolley cars were abandoned and we would travel by bus. In 1952, I graduated from the eighth grade at PS 9 Junior High (at the age of 14). Then, for five or six months, I went to Manual High Training School, a coed high school. I, reluctantly, had to attend Manual High because it was mandatory for students living in my zip code. *That's where I was assigned, until I got thrown out of there.*

The good news was that when I attended Manual High, I could walk to school because it was so close to home. At first, when I graduated from PS 9 Junior High, I thought I would be attending Brooklyn Technical High School, but they were too full; so, I ended up at Manual High. But, despite my reluctance, something good came out of it. That's where I first met Donald Haywoode. In 1953, there were only two "colored" people in the entire school - me and Donald. He would become my lifetime friend, and partner, in several singing groups.

A couple of days after I started attending classes at Manual High, I was in the classroom with a girl. She and I were hanging out together, just talking, when the door closed. It locked us in and we couldn't get it open. Soon after, we heard a voice say, "Open the door! What are you doing in there?" I don't know why the teacher thought I was up to 'no good'. Apparently, she assumed we were doing some hanky-panky, or that something immoral was going on …but she got the wrong idea. *The door closed accidentally, and we weren't doing anything wrong.* I was never given a chance to explain what happened. The teacher said, "Listen, we don't tolerate that kind of stuff in here." And, of course, to make matters worse, *the girl was white*.

So, after that incident, I was told, "We think you need to go to another school." With the teacher's recommendation, they transferred me to Boys High School, which was over in the "colored" area of Brooklyn. The good news was that, Boys High was the school I *really* wanted to attend, so it actually worked out in my favour. The only positive thing about Manual High was that it was where I met Donald. His reputation had preceded him, and I knew what a great musician he was. So, when I got ready to put my group together, The Troubadours, I went back and recruited him. Donald graduated from Manual High, the same year I graduated from Boys High.

When I was growing up, there were a lot of gangs in Brooklyn; and those guys were vicious. One of the gangs in my old neighbourhood - Red Hook - was the "Kovans"; and if you went down there into their territory, you were facing possible death. It was very rough. The neighbourhood I lived in was near the Fort Green Projects. The Chaplains had that area; and not too far from that was Bedford Stuyvesant, which was run by the "Bishops".

I was never in gangs. Fortunately, I managed to avoid that lifestyle. Because I was a well-known local singer, I could always get along with the guys, as long as I didn't mess with their women. Whenever I was in their "territory," if I started singing, I could avoid a confrontation. However, that was not too often because I knew where *not* to go, and I stayed away from those areas as much as possible. I couldn't avoid the gangs completely, though, because I went to Boys High and that was right in the middle of Bedford Stuyvesant – "Chaplains'" territory.

Some of the guys in the gangs also attended Boys High, but the good thing about it was the fact that I was a big wheel in the school. I was a popular singer and I was the "President of the 1956 Graduation Class." I was also the door monitor at the school, so everyone wanted to be on my good side. I used my position to my advantage and had strategized a strict "entrance" policy. *When you came late to school, you had to pay me a quarter*– I made a pretty good little income from that.

We had a very diverse cultural mix in Boys High School, which was totally amazing. Some of the smartest Jews used to come to Bedford Stuyvesant to attend classes. I believe that's why the grade averages there were so high. In fact, the highest percentage of the population at the school was Jewish students. They didn't attend Brooklyn Tech in *their* community, instead they came to Boys High in the *colored* community because the school was so highly-rated.

When I transferred to Boys High School I arrived there with a bit of a tainted reputation, but that soon changed. The other students thought I was a ladies' man, but it was just based on an innocent mistake. Those who knew the real story were saying things like, "This guy is coming over from the Manual High Training School. He's supposed to be this hot singer."

There was an introductory night for all the new students attending Boys High School and they asked me to sing. So, instinctively, I sang one of the hymns that I used to sing at church. When I started singing the hymn, the boys made fun of me. Then instead of singing the hymns, I started singing all these other "popular" songs in falsetto and the guys laughed like hell. They said things like, "What's this guy, a fag?" And they asked me, "Why are you singing like that, with that type of voice?"

It was unusual to hear guys sing falsetto, in those days before Eddie Kendrick made it popular to sing like that. So, they started yelling, "Get that fag off the stage!" They kind of laughed me off the stage, but I had caught the eye of Mrs. Bellavia, the Director of the music class at Boys High School. One part of the school music program was the chorus, which was called the "Melody Men." Ms. Bellavia recommended me to try out for the Melody Men, one of the most well-known high school boys' choirs in the state of New York. She gave me her business card, so I called her and she asked me if I would like to join the Melody Men. I said okay, and then I went to see her at her office; but I was embarrassed about those guys laughing at me and my high voice.

Ms. Bellavia told me, "We're going to put you into the tenors' section." And I said, "No, I want to be in the bass section." She said, "No, with your voice, you cannot be a bass singer." So, I went to join the group as a tenor and when I heard someone that sounded like Mario Lanza, I said, "That's not for me." And then I walked down the hall and I heard someone singing soprano. I went over, knocked on the door, and said, "I came here to audition." The teacher said, "You are a man," and I said, "Ya, but I sing like that."

The All-City Choir was a coed choir. I went in there, joined the chorus, and started singing with the Sopranos. I stayed there for three years, until I graduated from Boys High School. When my mother came to the school to hear me sing, she was so embarrassed. She said, "I came over here and my son is singing with the girls." I guess I had forgotten to tell her that.

When I sang with the school choir, I started working with great singers. I had met Jerome Ramos (Romie) who would later become the lead singer of the Velours. It was so ironic because a few years prior, Romie and I had actually lived on the same street, next door to each other. Up until then, it hadn't occurred to me that I had previously known Romie or that he had lived next door to me. *I guess I was too young to remember where he lived.* We didn't realize it for years, until I happened to walk into Boys High School in the choir and I saw him there.

We immediately struck up a relationship. One day, when we were discussing our childhood, I told Romie that I had lived at 530 Dean Street, and Romie told me that he had lived at 532 Dean Street. We agreed that there had been a lot of fun times playing in our old neighbourhood, even though Romie and I weren't really "friends" then, and despite the fact that his brother Arthur had shot me years earlier. We both had a good laugh about it.

At Boys High School, I scored fifth highest in my graduation class. I graduated with about a 90 percent grade average. I could have gone to any college I chose, but I was now heading down a different path. Soon after graduation, I got a hit record; so instead, I went on the road as an entertainer. I had graduated from Boys High School in July 1956. Two months later, in September 1956, I was on the road touring with the Velours and *Ray Charles*.

SIX

THE PERILS OF MY CHILDHOOD

When I was a young child, I was very sickly. I used to catch everything. I had rheumatic fever and it was really bad. In fact, it almost killed me. Obviously, it didn't kill me because I'm still here; but it did destroy my eyes. It is one of the reasons why my eyes are so bad today, not because of my age. The heat of the fever fused the blood vessels in the back of my eyes under my retina. The entire area in back of my eyes is black. I can only see through the peripheral, so I have peripheral vision. The middle of my eyes is just total scar tissue, and it's been like that ever since I was six years old. When I go to the hospital now, the doctors are shocked about the condition of my eyes. They say, "My God!" But, obviously, I have adapted quite well. *Unfortunately, nothing can help with my vision except new eyes.*

Because I was always sick, I would be home from school a lot, sometimes alone. When I was six-years-old, Romie's brother, Arthur Ramos had come to my house. I opened the door for him and he said, "Listen John, I was just at my uncle's house and he had these hunting guns." Arthur's uncle, Mr. Herd, had the largest black funeral parlour in the Brooklyn area at the time. And Arthur had gotten a hold of one of his guns. When Arthur came to my house, he said, "Look! I got this pistol!" When he said 'look,' I turned to look at him, and suddenly I could see this fire coming out at me. Arthur had shot the gun. I turned my head and the bullet grazed the side of my head. It chopped a piece of my ear off and got stuck up into the wall. My blood started gushing out. This had happened while my mother was working. She was the manager of the paint department at Loesers and Namms Department Store in Downtown Brooklyn, on Fulton Street.

My aunt was at home, in another room. She didn't work, rather she looked after the house and cooked for our family. When the gun went off the people next door heard it first. I had left the door open when I let Arthur in and the neighbours ran into our apartment. They said, "What the hell was that!" Then they saw my ear bleeding and ran out to call the ambulance to take me to the hospital, because they thought it was more serious than it actually was. Fortunately, it was just a graze. The bullet had ripped a little piece of my ear off, and that's where the blood was coming from.

My mother arrived at the hospital in what seemed like a matter of minutes. When she saw me, she started to scream. The doctor bandaged me up and gave me some shots. They told my mother that I should sue Mr Herd because he shouldn't have guns where young kids could get their hands on them. *I was six-years-old, and Arthur was about nine-years-old at the time.* But my mother said, "No, the Lord wouldn't allow that." Nowadays, my mother *would* probably sue. But back then she said, "No, the Lord wouldn't allow that; just forget about it. He's alive, so that's fine."

So, that happened and it kind of shut me down for a while. I didn't want to go out to play with the other children in the neighbourhood. I just watched them from my window. I was in pretty bad shape for a while from the effects of the Rheumatic Fever and the gunshot; but I eventually got over that. I was a bit nervous for a couple of years, but it still didn't stop me from joining the Boy Scouts and participating in other group activities. My mother, aunt and uncle continued to comfort me and helped me to regain my courage.

I had a long career as a Boy Scout. My mother was a den mother for the Cub Scouts. First, I joined the Cub Scouts when I was about six-years-old, at which time I was in troop 219 Brooklyn. I remember those days very fondly. Then I became a Boy Scout. It was a lot of fun when we used to go to Boy Scout Camp Minisink in Upstate New York.

Later, I became an Explorer Scout and then I finished my scouting career as a Life Scout. I was one of the most decorated Boy Scouts in Brooklyn. The highest rank you can achieve is Eagle Scout. When you become an Eagle Scout, you are given a college scholarship. The Merit Badge that you achieve before the Eagle Scout is the Life Scout. Since I was a Life Scout, all I needed to do was go up to 10-mile River Camp and earn two Merit Badges - swimming and lifesaving - to receive my Eagle Scout rank. I would then be given an automatic college scholarship.

Every time I had to go up to 10-mile River Camp to try to earn my final two merit badges, the scout master would throw me in the water. There were water moccasins in the water. I was so terrified that I went straight to the bottom. I missed the opportunity to become an Eagle Scout, but I became a proud Life Scout. I was one of the few recipients of that rank, so The Boy Scouts of America gave me what is called the "Guard and Country Medal." It is one of the highest awards you can get in the Boy Scouts. When I received that award, I was 16-years-old and attending Boys High School.

I was an only child and my mother was very protective of me and careful about who she dated. As a matter of fact, she didn't get married until sixteen years after my father died.

One day, when my mother came to the scout meeting, my Scoutmaster, William Adams, saw her and they started talking. She was comfortable around him and felt he was a good role model for me. The next thing I knew, he was visiting my mother at our house. So, I said, "Mom, what's my scout master doing at our house?" She just smiled and told me that they were friends. The next thing I knew they were dating, and then soon afterwards, she told me they were getting married. I said, "That's good!" So, they got married and then they moved uptown to St. Johns Place and, of course, took me with them.

When my mother and I moved, we had to leave my aunt and uncle. I was very disheartened because they were my family, the family I had been with all my young life. When my mother remarried, I was a teenager, about fifteen-years-old and she was in her forties. Ever since we moved to New York, my aunt had been doing *all* the cooking. I told my mother I didn't want to go live with her and my stepfather because she couldn't cook. *That was really the main reason I didn't want to move. My mother's cooking skills were so bad that she would have to call my aunt for cooking instructions.*

Nine years after my uncle joined the family, we moved. I was very disheartened when we moved, because I had to leave my uncle and aunt downtown at 530 Dean Street. Seeing my uncle when he came home from work, had been a bright spot of my day.

It's interesting how fate intervenes in your life when you least expect it. I believe that things are not by coincidence, they are predestined. We were still very young when our paths crossed for the second time, but a Higher Power had brought us back together when the time was right. I didn't realize that Romie had been a former childhood acquaintance, until years later when we were in the high school chorus. I recognized him and said, "You're the guy who used to live next door!" I wasn't allowed to play with him then, though.

Romie's father was Puerto Rican, his mother Silvea was black. There were about six kids in the Ramos family. The two I knew best were Romie and his brother Arthur, who was two years older than him. Romie was a year older than me and Arthur was three years older than me. Romie's older brother Arthur was always hanging out in the neighbourhood and getting into mischief. Because of his antics, I got shot.

The last year I went to Boys High School, Romie was still there. Arthur had already graduated the year before I started attending the school.

After he left Boys High, Arthur went straight to Los Angeles and started to work with the Inkspots. He was with the group until about 2007. Arthur was a classical-type singer with a big voice, he was amazing. Romie had a kind of doo-wop voice; he was good, but he didn't sing like Arthur.

My life changed extensively after Arthur Ramos shot me. My mother, trying to keep me safe from harm, had forbidden me from associating with Arthur and Romie and all the other neighbourhood children. So, from that point on, starting at the age of six, I spent all my time either in the house or at Boy Scouts. While I stayed at home, I found things that I could do to entertain myself. Since I was an only child, I learned to be creative.

Crossword puzzles were always a good pastime and after reflecting back, I am sure my fondness for doing them, to this day, reflected on how well I did in school. I also liked to collect trains, not just toy trains, but pictures of "real" trains. I would write to the train companies and ask them to send me their catalogues with pictures of the trains, which I would cut out and collect. There were quite a few companies back then, including: Central Pacific, Chicago and North Western, Northern Pacific, Southern Pacific and Union Pacific. When my mother saw how much I loved trains, she bought me a Lionel Train set.

She also bought me a pool table – I guess she felt that playing pool would give me a little physical exercise since I had to stay indoors. And, I cannot forget my radio. I loved to listen to the comedy shows on the radio – “Amos and Andy” was particularly funny. And the cowboy shows like “Lone Ranger” were very exciting.

Although I was not a big fan of the piano, when I thought no one was listening, I enjoyed singing along to the tunes that were on the rollers. So, although I was pretty much a loner, I kept very busy.

SEVEN

TOURING

My first experience, as a singer on tour in America was in 1956, when I was 18-years-old. As soon as I told my mother I was going on the road, she told me I had to move out of the house. Everything happened at once. Right after I went to have my hair processed for the first time, I went home and my mother asked me, "What did you do!?" I told her that I went to get my hair done. She said, "You can't walk around looking like that! How are you going to go to church looking like that?" I said, "Mom I ain't going to church no more!" She was furious and told me, "That's it, out of the house!" She threw me right out of the house. "Get out!" I had to go back and live with my aunt and uncle downtown. She said, "I ain't having that! You looking like that… it's disgraceful!" And the other guys' mothers did the same to them. They all said, "Listen here, you ain't going to church no more, so you are going to have to get out of this house!" It was unbelievable.

When I processed my hair, I didn't have much hair on my head to begin with, but I had to do it so I could look like the other singers in the group. We all went to the hairdresser together and had our hair processed at the same time. A guy named Woody used to do processing for $5. The process was like a mixture of lye and white potatoes. He used to mix it up, apply it on our hair and comb it through our hair to straighten it out. It made some waves and made our hair shiny and pretty, but it used to burn like hell. We braved it out because we wanted to look good. I guess I figured that I was grown and it was time to move out anyway; but I didn't have a real plan. Lucky for me, things eventually started falling into place and soon I would be on the road touring with our group, the Velours.

When we first formed our group, we were known as the Troubadours. The Troubadours didn't tour, but we became well-known locally, in New York. We performed often at the Apollo Amateur Night Talent Show. The last time we appeared at the Apollo Theatre as the Troubadours, Nat King Cole performed there as the featured artist. We went on stage and got so much applause that we thought we had won the talent show. But, a few minutes later, another group that had been hanging out next door at the bar said, "Let's go make some drinking money." They had a hit record out at the time called "Darlene," which was only known in Harlem. They came out onstage, performed, and won first place. They beat us out and took the prize money away from us. As a gesture, though, they handed us $10 and kept $25. *I guess it could have been worse.*

The Troubadours performed regularly at the Apollo, but the Velours toured. The Velours' first release was "My Love Come Back." it made some noise and gave us a little prominence around New York. So, people had heard about us; but by the time "Can I Come Over Tonight" dropped, they were ready for us. We became an overnight sensation.

<><><><><><>

Back in those days, there were two promoters who had tours. There was Bill Weinberg's tour that the Velours used to go on in the South and there was Irving Feld, whose tours used to travel out West. Irving Feld travelled all through the West and his tours were racially-mixed. Paul Anka and Jackie Wilson would tour along the East Coast and the Midwest with him, but they didn't go through the South.

The Velours' first tour was with all Black performers. It was a total "Blues" tour with Ray Charles and his band. The tour was just a wonderful journey and one of the key things that propelled our career in the entertainment business.

The tour bus picked up all the groups in Harlem, New York at The Apollo Theatre. Most of the groups performed at The Apollo on a regular basis and they all had easy access to meet there. Ray Charles had been performing at The Apollo that night when we met up to leave on the Southern Tour. He had a big band - about twenty members – as well as his three backup singers from Brooklyn. Ray named them the Raelettes, but they were originally known as the Cookies. We also had Mickey and Sylvia (*Love is Strange*) on our first tour. They were co-stars with Ray Charles. Plus, we had a blues singer named Annie Lori, and also The Moonglows. That entire experience was amazing, and working with Harvey Fuqua and the Moonglows was awesome.

Harvey Fuqua was an American rhythm-and-blues singer, songwriter, record producer, and record label executive. He founded the seminal R&B/doo-wop group the Moonglows in the 1950s. He is notable as one of the key figures in the development of the Motown label in Detroit,

Michigan. His group gave Marvin Gaye a start in his music career. Fuqua and his wife at the time, Gwen Gordy, distributed the first Motown hit single, Barrett Strong's "Money (That's What I Want)," on their record label, Anna Records. Fuqua later sold Anna Records to Gwen's brother Berry Gordy and became a songwriter and executive at Motown. He was the nephew of Charlie Fuqua of the Ink Spots and the uncle of the filmmaker Antoine Fuqua. (Harvey Fuqua died July 6, 2010 at the age of 8o).

On the tour, we also had Bo Didley - a blues singer, Rickey Nelson, Big Joe Turner, Larry Williams, Roy Brown and Nancy Brown. We even had two gay singers - Charlie and Ray. In every city that we went to, the gay fans were sitting there waiting for Charlie and Ray and they would meet up with them and bring them to the dressing room. Those guys were doing some awful stuff in there and the straight guys on the tour would be saying, "You want to see what they're doing?" *I didn't want to see what they were doing*. Those guys were unbelievable. *Can you imagine all of us on tour together? And I was just a kid, nineteen-years-old!*

Some nights, the two tour groups - Bill Weinberg and Irving Feld - might be appearing close to each other and all the performers would meet and talk about how their shows were going. They had all these issues between the various acts on the Feld tour, and we had all these blues singers appearing on the Weinberg shows talking about everything imaginable, making history together.

The Weinberg group toured everywhere, not just in the South; but even as far north as Washington DC. Along the way, particularly on the southern tours, hundreds of people opened their houses – similar to a "bed and breakfast" - to the bands. There weren't many options for "colored folks" back in those days. A. Gatston had the largest black hotel in Atlanta and there were a few other Black-owned hotels where the Black headliners would stay, and we would stay around the corner from there in designated homes. The band members would make arrangements ahead of time with the people we stayed with - "hosts." A lot of the guys got to know these people because they were traveling around touring all the time. The hosts would always have food prepared for us when we arrived. In the morning, before the tour bus picked us up, the hosts would tell us to come down for breakfast. They would be serving something like hominy grits and chitterlings and they said, "Have some!" Then we said, "We don't eat no chitterlings!" And they used to laugh at us. Or sometimes, it would be chopped liver, hog maws and all that southern food that we "northerners" were not accustomed to.

If we had a hit in New York, people in the South didn't hear it because, in the '50s, hits were regional. There was no radio - as we know it today, no video or entertainment television shows, and no internet to spread the word or promote the songs. So, when we got on the stage to perform our songs, it was the first time most of the people in the audience heard them. The point is, that taught us to be "entertainers" in the *true* sense of the word, because we had to do something to make the people smile. It was a wonderful experience, which taught us how to be "real" entertainers. That's why when we went back home after those tours, we were better performers than any other group in New York City. In a sense, it all came full circle, because by having a big hit in

New York, we were selected to go on the tour and that enabled us to grow.

People all over the country began to know about The Velours. Our popularity and showmanship would make us a star attraction. Then other artists started asking us to go on tour with them. We used to work with Chuck Willis quite often.

Alan Best out of Philadelphia was our manager. He also managed the Turbans. Jerry Winston, the owner of Onyx Records, our record company at the time, knew Alan and he had referred him to us. Alan came to see us perform and he liked what he saw and told Jerry, "Okay I'll manage them!" During that time, touring was our only income stream because there were never any residuals from record sales.

Jerry Winston also had a label call Mardi Gras Records, the largest Latin company in New York. "Everybody Likes to Cha Cha Cha" was one of their big hits. It would have been nice if the recording artists got paid for the songs they recorded and if songwriters got paid for the songs they wrote; but back then, that wasn't the case. Only the people making the records - the "white-owned" record companies - were in a position to make any money from record sales. But, most of the record companies didn't make any money either, and thus there was a large turnover of record companies going out of business.

When we made a record, the record companies would send them to the stores on "consignment." In other words, the records would be sent to the stores, but no money would exchange hands until they were actually sold. But if the stores didn't sell the records, they would send them back to the record companies without paying for them. So, the record companies might have sent out a million records throughout the country and the stores might not have sold any, then the artist might say, "Where's the money?" And the record company would say, "There isn't any." And to make matters worse, the record company had to pay the studio to record the songs, pay the manufacturer to press the records, and pay the shipping company (both ways) without collecting a dime.

That's what happened to the Velours. Between 1956 and 1958 we had recorded five records and we weren't getting any residuals from the record sales. Jerry Winston called us in to his office one day and we went downstairs and he opened up his garage and said, "See all these records in here that I can't sell? There's your money!" And, soon after, Jerry closed the company down because he had no money.

Berry Gordy had the same problem when he started Motown. He would ship out records and the stores would send them back to him, instead of money. If it wasn't for Phil Chess, who bailed him out and lent him money to keep going, there would probably be no Motown Records today.

In England, it's different. If anyone wants to order records, they have to buy them "prepaid," not on consignment. The record stores can't just order records and send them back. Therefore, when a record company ships records, they are already sold, so they don't have a problem with returns, because there is no "consignment option" in England.

Donald Haywoode, the guy I met at Manual Training High School, wrote all the hits for The Velours. He got *no* publishing on any of those songs. It was non-existent back in those days – in the '50s and '60s and most of the '70s. There was no money from record sales, the only money we got as artists was what we made on tour. No record royalties, nor songwriter's royalties. Publishing and all that didn't come along until Sam Cooke. He was possibly the first modern black performer and composer to attend to the business side of his musical career. Sam Cooke founded both a record label and a publishing company as an extension of his career as a singer and composer. Later, when Ray Charles started making country songs like "I Can't Stop Loving You," he said, "I want to start my own publishing company," and then a trend began.

The Velours were just recording to become famous and to get the girls. We thought that was enough for us. After all, we were just young guys. We were having a great time and we were not yet planning our futures. My mother used to ask me, "How much money did you make?" And I said, "Ma, do you know how many girls I have?" She was not very happy with my response.

There were two buses on our first tour. They had one big Greyhound bus for the headliner acts and a smaller bus for the band and the groups. Of course, The Velours rode in the small bus. Many of the guys who rode in the big bus brought their wives with them. We thought that was nice… the other guys traveling with their wives…*yeah, right*.

As the tour went on, we kept hearing these guys talking about different women. So, I'm thinking, *I can't believe these guys... they're with their wives and they keep talking about other women.* We couldn't understand what was going on and as the tour continued some of the guys' wives started leaving, saying things like: "I am tired, I am sick of this!" The couples were all fighting and the wives started leaving. By the time we got to a certain point on the tour, all the wives had gone back home. When we arrived in Atlanta, we saw these "other" women standing there. All those headliners had their girlfriends waiting for them down South. They had been doing this for years and it was probably a regular routine for them. They knew their wives were going to leave and the girlfriends were going to be waiting. That was one of the experiences I remember vividly. I thought, *Boy! Can you believe that?*

Then, during the time that we were touring, I had a heart-breaking experience. It really crushed me. I had been going with Lucy since we were 12-years-old and we even went to church together. In fact, we spent almost all our time together. We were planning to get married one day and have children and build a great life together. We were very close, but we never had sex because we were just waiting until we got married.

So, the Velours were out on a tour for about two weeks. Whenever we wanted to make a phone call, there was always just one phone available for the black people to use. So, we had to get in a long line to use the phone. I was waiting in the line to call Lucy because I hadn't spoken to her in two weeks. When I finally got a phone, I dialled Lucy's number.

I called her house in Brooklyn. No one answered the phone, so I called again. Her mother answered and said, “Who is this?” I said Mrs. Howes, it's John.” She said, “Hello John, how are you?” I said, “Could I speak to Lucy?” She said, “She doesn't want to speak to you.” And I said, “What do you mean, she doesn't want to speak to me?” She said, “She’s got a new boyfriend.” I said, “How come she has a new boyfriend? She's been going with me for about ten years and we've been together almost every day for ten years. I've only been gone for 2 weeks.” Mrs Howes then told me, “Well, she doesn’t want to talk to you, she has a boyfriend.” And she hung up the phone.

I started crying. Then, all the guys started laughing and pointing at me. Someone yelled, “Hey, look at this guy crying!” And everybody started laughing again. So, Bobby Lesson, the lead singer of the Moonglows came to me and said, “Hey, what's your name?” I said, “John.” He asked me, “What's the matter?” I said, “My girlfriend left me.” He said, “Well, call another one.” I said, “I don't have another one.” He said, “What! You ain't got no girlfriend?” He said, “Hey guys, he don't got no other girlfriend.” They thought that was the funniest thing.

I soon got over Lucy and started dating other girls. The Velours were gaining a lot of notoriety up along the East Coast, particularly when “Can I Come Over Tonight?” was released. I heard that our records were being played on the radio in Boston, but I had never been there.

The first time I went to Boston was in the ‘60s. A friend of mine, who used to sing with the Platters, joined up with Herb Reed there. *Herb had moved to the Boston area, after the success of The Platters. He was a founding member of the Platters and the only member who sang on all of the approximately 400 songs recorded by the group. Reed, who was the last surviving original member of the group, died in Danvers Massachusetts in June 2012 at the age of 83.*

I went to see the Platters perform and my friend took me over to Estelle's Lounge. It was a nightclub on Tremont Street in Boston's "Roxbury" section, near where many of Boston's Black socialites resided. Roxbury was an amazing place – and Estelle's Nightclub was phenomenal. At one time, Estelle's used to be the hotbed of entertainment where the list of "who's who" Jazz, Blues and R & B singers performed.

The 50s and the 60s were phenomenal years for me. That's when my whole world opened up and my passion to be an entertainer became heightened. *That's when I realized that I would never look back.*

EIGHT

LEARNING THE WAYS

Our group lived in New York and the first gig on our tour was in Greenville, North Carolina. It was a long, but exciting bus ride. The first night, when we got down to the theatre, the band was setting up and it looked very strange with the way they were arranging everything. Instead of the typical square-type stage at the front of the theatre, there was a long stage, like a runway. On one side, you had seats and on the other side, you had Standing Room. Then the band was setting up at the back leading toward the stage, not positioned on either side, but from wall-to-wall. It was like a "T" formation.

I went up to the stagehands and said, "Hey listen, how come you guys are setting up like that?" They said, "This is how we do it down here. We sing to the wall, we sing straight to the wall; and when you are finished singing, if the promoter is white, first you bow to the white people, who are sitting down and then you bow to the black people, who are dancing at the other side of the stage. If it's the other way around, with black promoters, which is very rare, the black people will sit down and you would go to them first; and then the white people second, but that very rarely happens."

So anyway, we started working these shows and touring at all these venues. The places were packed, and people enjoyed themselves. It was really great.

The strange thing about being down South was that I was a novelty because, during the time of our tour, I had red hair. One day, Donald and I started walking around the streets with our new "conked" hairdos; and these white people were looking at us, saying, "Man look at that redhead Nigger." They used to repeat the word Nigger Nigger Nigger Nigger. I heard myself being called Nigger so much, that when the white people came to ask me, "What's your name?" I proudly told them, "My name is John 'Nigger' Cheatdom." After all, they kept calling me Nigger and I was just being humble.

When we toured, we were dressed to impress. We wore nice suede shoes and we always dressed impeccably, especially when we were traveling down to the southern states going to: North Carolina, South Carolina, Georgia, and Alabama. Everywhere we went, whenever we stopped in one of the cafes, or in one of the big roadway diners - a Motorway Café, a Howard Johnson restaurant, or a place like that - we had to go around the back and stand in a line. Then some rude white lady would open the door and say, "What you boys want?" And, quite often, we had to stand in the mud with our nice suede shoes on. It was horrible. That's how we got fed back in the day. Everybody on the bus had to stand outside the café in a line, no matter what the weather.

Somebody on the Southern Tour was always getting locked up, everywhere we went. One of the blues singers was always getting into a fight and the cops were always there.

We weren't used to that kind of blatant racism, but we quickly fell into the routine. Coming from New York, we'd never seen that type of treatment before…*I must admit surviving in the South grew me up pretty fast.* Even when I went down to West Virginia to visit my grandparents, it wasn't considered the "deep" south. West Virginia was segregated, but it wasn't *that* bad because at least we could go into the shops and stuff like that.

So, we were very surprised about the racism and the disrespect that we received. The strangest thing about it was, even though, as well-known as our group was in New York, we realized then that music in those days was regional. If you had a hit in New York, people in the rest of the country had probably never even heard it. And that was the case with the Velours. We were singing on stage and people had never heard any of the songs we were singing, but we looked good and we used to have all the girls screaming. The promoter, Bill Weinberg was pleased about our performances. He told us, "You guys were good and you're only going to get better as time goes on."

Our record company, Onyx, had appointed the Turban's manager Alan Best from Philadelphia as our road manager. He liked the act so he put us on the regular roster and we got a lot of shows. The bus tours were tough, though. There were so many guys who had so many bad habits. We'd leave New York and then we would drive all night. Our first show would be, let's say in North Carolina. We probably did about seven shows on a tour, but we were not going to them all in a row. After North Carolina, for instance, we would probably go up to Virginia, then to Tennessee, then back to North Carolina. It was ridiculous. We'd say, "Why can't we do all the North Carolina shows together?" But, it didn't work that way, they'd have to spread it out.

It was some tour, I'm telling you. But it was gratifying. We learned a lot, especially working with the Moonglows and Harvey Fuqua – those people taught us so much about the music business. By the time the Velours got back home to New York, after touring, we were well-seasoned entertainers. We were so polished - it was ridiculous. We went in there and just tore the place apart. That's why we used to work at the Apollo so much - we were a big favourite.

We started working at the Apollo Theatre in Harlem, doing six shows a day, forty-two shows a week. There were twelve acts on a show, and each act did about three songs. Because we were doing so many shows a day, as soon as we did our first gig, we decided that, instead of going back home every day, we would check into a hotel in Harlem. We stayed up there for the entire week so we could get some rest, and, of course, because the girls were there.

The up-and-coming acts, like ours, stayed around the corner from Harlem's famous Theresa Hotel, either at The Grambion Hotel or Mills Plaza. Later, when we started earning more money, like Ray Charles, we moved to the Theresa. After we performed, we would grab some girls bring them back to the hotel, do what we had to do and then run back between shows.

Life was moving fast and I got exposed to many things, but through the Grace of God, I never got "hooked on drugs." When we first started singing back in the '50s we were young guys, so we didn't drink and the other guys we met thought that was very funny. We knew that in order to survive in the entertainment business, we really had to stay grounded and strong. We witnessed so much strange behaviour and had all kinds of experiences and all types of influences… some good, some not so good.

Some place in New Jersey, we were off-stage waiting to perform. I was standing there on the right checking out Roy Brown, who was standing near me. Joe Turner walked over to me, and then he pointed at Roy, and said, "Hey boy, he's fantastic. You were looking 'cause he's cool, but I'm the king." *The rivalry between the artists was unbelievable, but the people loved them.* Then Joe Turner pulled out a bottle of bourbon and told me "Here, have some of this." I turned him down. He took a swig and then returned it to his hip pocket before going on stage.

After we were in the business a while, we would hang out at the clubs and start drinking beer. Then some of the other guys would start smoking joints. We didn't smoke weed – it never appealed to us - we just drank beer. The first time I witnessed someone doing hard drugs, was when we started working at the Apollo. Prior to that, we had never seen a real junkie - a real heroin addict - until we met Errol Wade with the Cadillacs.

Errol was the first one. He was a good-looking pretty boy, the nicest guy you would ever want to meet in your life. We came to work one day and saw him standing there. He was backstage in a stupor, looking dirty and dishevelled. We didn't know what had happened to him. I asked, "Errol, are you okay?" But he was gone… spaced out. So, I asked the other guys in the group, "What happened to Errol?"

Somebody turned around and said, "Heroin." Soon after that, his music career was finished. Errol had a great family – a beautiful wife and children. It was really sad. He was the first casualty that we would witness first-hand. Fortunately, the Velours never ever got into that. There was another incident – I think the guy's name was Billy Bailey. He sang with the Heartbeats. He was another casualty of the business. I heard that Billy got poisoned by a groupie.

The entertainment business was fantastic, but it was a very slippery slope – especially for newbies like The Velours. The drug dealers were always around sniffing out the money, and plenty of the guys, who we knew, were indulging. You might call it, "good versus evil." We were kids having a good time, but for the most part, we didn't drink. We didn't smoke weed or do any drugs because that never appealed to us. When we met all the other groups, like the Dells and the Spaniels, those guys drank hard liquor. We started out just drinking beer, but later when we hung out with the older guys, we gradually acquired a taste for bourbon.

The interesting thing about it was my parents, my grand-dad, my uncles and everybody else in West Virginia were heavy drinkers; they would drink bourbon. When they used to come out of the coal mines, they smelled quite bad. My uncles and my granddad built a shed outside the house, so they could go into the shed and take a shower. Then they sat around and drank their bourbon. I used to sit there and watch them and thought, *"Oh, I can't wait till I get older to drink some of that."*

I eventually became a bourbon drinker, also. That is my favourite beverage. But, in the beginning, I just drank beer. Then, I used to drink a little bit of "bourbon with ginger on the rocks." Then, the more the guys in the group hung out, the more we started drinking. We never became alcoholics, but we became heavy drinkers, especially when we were hanging out after the shows. I would always say, *Alcoholics drink to live, heavy drinkers live to drink.* We were "heavy drinkers" and, I will admit, we used to drink quite often. But most of the guys in the group were able to go through life normally and we never missed our gigs. I guess you can say we weren't "sloppy drinkers." In fact, we got better and better at our craft because we worked constantly.

There was always something new to learn at the shows. The older guys loved to teach us "pups" what to do and how to survive, although sometimes we had to fend for ourselves and learn by our own mistakes. I recall working with a white New York vocal group called The Mello Kings, they sang *Tonight Tonight*. Their reputation was spreading and we got booked on a show with them, thinking we would 'kick their ass'. When we were in the dressing room, one of the guys from the group came in wearing a sharp blue tuxedo with braided trim. When he walked in, all the guys seeing his outfit mumbled s***. But, it was too late, we already told the promoter we'd *close* the show. That was the biggest mistake we made in our lives. The Mello Kings tore the place apart. *We couldn't follow them – but we had no choice.* You can bet that we never made that mistake again. From that day on, we would always check out the enemy that appeared on tour with us.

Later, when we did the Alan Freed shows with Jerry Lee Lewis and Larry Williams, we made sure we performed *before* they did. Larry Williams sang "short Fat Fanny" and he used to jump off the piano and then run into the audience. Larry, who was a Black version of Jerry Lee Lewis, looked exactly like me. People used to call him my brother - we were the same height. When I met Larry, I looked at him and laughed and he looked at me and said, "Who's your momma?"

I have many great memories of those times during my early career spent with the Velours.

NINE

STARTING ALL OVER AGAIN

The Velours disbanded in 1961. In 1966, I got lucky when I met a singer named Gary Gant. He was the leader of a group called the Invitations, also from Brooklyn, and they were working in England. They had been touring in England and Gary asked me if the Velours would like to go there to do some shows. I said, "Well, I am married now and raising a family. And, besides that, I don't have a group, we broke up and I haven't spoken to the guys in four years." So, he said, "Why don't you call them up and have a word with them and just see if the guys would like to do something overseas." Gary continued, "Maybe you're married and you work in a post office or go to college and all that, but maybe the other guys are bored, and maybe they might want to do something else. Why don't you give them a call?" I told him okay.

From 1961 to 1965, I hadn't been singing at all. I went to Brooklyn College during the day and worked in the Post Office on the midnight shift. Because I did so well in high school, later on, in 1961, when I stopped touring, I worked in Brooklyn and I was able to enrol in nearby Brooklyn College. At that time, Brooklyn College was basically a Jewish college. They had 2000 Jews and about nine Blacks in attendance, when I was going there. You couldn't get accepted at

Brooklyn College unless you had at least 85-90 average. But I just walked in and registered. It was no problem for me to get accepted. I studied music education because I had planned to become a music teacher.

I was married and just being a "normal" husband and father; but raising my children did not fulfill me. I was miserable. When I met my wife, she lived in the Marcy projects in Brooklyn – the same projects that Jay-Z came from. Jacqueline was a member of one of our fan clubs - the Velour Queens. She was always around, loved The Velours and fell in love with me. We dated, but at the time, I had a lot of women. All the other guys in the group were getting married and my mother kept asking me, "John, when are you getting married? You're making all these babies and you're embarrassing the family. Shape up!" She was right, I already had two daughters with two different mothers. So, I told my mother, "Okay." Jacqueline was great, straight, smart. We had a big wedding at the church in 1963 when I was twenty-five years old.

My wife, Jacqueline, and I had two children – a girl named Kantata and a boy named Kevin. Kevin lives in Winston-Salem, North Carolina, where he manages a phone company. He has two children. Kantata lives in Temecula, California with her husband and two boys. She is managing director for Morgan Stanley. Formerly she worked in their office in the World Trade Center, when they occupied the top two floors. A year before the planes hit, Kantata was transferred to Los Angeles. Fortunately, she wasn't in New York during the tragic event, but tragically, all her friends at Morgan Stanley's New York office died.

I have two older daughters, who both live in Brooklyn, New York and both are very dedicated to their churches. Faustina, my oldest daughther was born in 1958, when I was twenty-seven years old. My second oldest daughter, Valdina was born in 1960, and works for one of the largest banks in New York City.

Jacqueline currently lives in Winston-Salem, North Carolina, so she can be close to our son Kevin and his two children. She and I had been together for four years, before I went to London in 1967. When we got married, I had promised Jacqueline that I would quit show business and just be a working husband; but when Gary Gant called me and said, "Let's go on tour", I was ready.

A number of the things that made me realize how unhappy I was came full circle when I witnessed the progress that was being made by new upcoming groups. Little Anthony and the Imperials were my students back in the day. I helped them with their harmonies and showed them some dance moves. I also gave them advice about some of the ins and outs of the entertainment business. When they started their group and recorded "Going Out of My Head," "Hurt so Bad" and all their other hit songs, they had asked me to join the group. I told them, "No, I am retired now." Then I saw them on TV - on the Ed Sullivan Show, and I was very upset.

While I was a Postal Worker, I was home being a good husband and father. Every now and then, I would give advice to some of the younger guys in the neighbourhood. And, somehow, the word got out that I was "coaching" groups. So, a lot of guys would call me and ask me to help them put their groups together. During my marriage, that was the extent of my musical involvement. Coaching kept my foot in the door of the entertainment business, but I was no longer in a starring role or touring. Many of the groups I coached were becoming big stars and I was becoming more and more miserable. I told Jacqueline, "The next time someone calls me to do a show, I'm gone because I can't take this." Jacqueline and I both knew that once I started performing again, our marriage was finished.

As soon as I heard from Gary Gant, I called Romie and Donald, and said, "We are gonna do this because, if we don't, our life is going to pass us by." So, I retired from the Post Office. Romie, Donald and I left New York, came to England, and never looked back. And, of course, all our wives divorced us. *Nearly five decades later, I am still touring and I am still happy that I made that decision.*

First, I called Donald. He said, "John, I'm so glad to hear your voice. What's up?" I told him that I got a call from this guy, Gary, who's talking about us going to England. And he said, "Wow that sounds good, but you know I'm married to Delores. We have a daughter and I got a pharmacy job, so I'm pretty set. I don't know if I want to do that."

And then I called Romie; we hadn't talked in years because we had a bad experience. Actually, it was one of the worst experiences that we had with Romie. When we were touring, we had been invited to Alan Freed's Rock and Roll show. It was a great honor and a great opportunity. Albert James "Alan" Freed also known as Moondog, was an American disc jockey. He became internationally known for promoting the mix of blues, country, and rhythm and blues music on the radio in the United States and Europe - all under the name of 'rock and roll'. His career was destroyed by the payola scandal that hit the broadcasting industry in the early 1960s.This was to be the last big Rock and Roll show that Alan Freed had. It was being held in Brooklyn at the Fox Theatre...and The Velours were invited to perform.

That night, everyone but Romie showed up at the Fox Theatre. There was supposed to be Charles Moffett, Jerome "Romie" Ramos, John Pearson, Donald Haywoode and me. I was First Tenor, Donald was Second Tenor, Charles was Bass, and Pete was Baritone. We had two lead singers. When we did up-tempo songs, Donald sang them and Romie sang the ballads. So, when Donald sang lead, Romie sang second tenor. That night, however, at the Fox Theatre, Donald had to do lead because Romie didn't show up.

Early on I was gaining a reputation for discovering the right talent for the groups I worked with. In fact, later in life, I was being referred to as the "Glue" for my ability to keep us all together. I first met Donald at Manual Training High School. When he joined the group, he sang sometimes; but he was also a piano player and a great arranger. Basically, I recruited him into the group to do second tenor with me and to do the group's arrangements. But he never thought about doing any lead singing, so until we started actually working together and he started actually singing those songs, he had not developed his voice. That night at the Fox Theatre, however, Donald stepped up to the plate. His great musical talent took over "center-stage" and he proved that he was unstoppable.

The Fox Theatre originally opened on August 31, 1928 with Janet Gaynor in "Street Angel". It had 4,305 seats. Interior decorations were in a mix of Spanish Baroque, with Marine motifs. The proscenium was 50 feet wide, the stage 39 feet deep. It was equipped with The Wurlitzer organ that was one of five in the country known as "Fox Specials." For many years, the Fox was a centrepiece of "Downtown Brooklyn," ultimately becoming a popular concert venue for rock 'n' roll shows emceed by Murray Kaufman (Murray the "K"). The theatre's popularity waned and in 1970, the Fox Theatre was demolished.

The show that Alan Freed asked us to perform at, had everybody who was famous in show business at the time. It had the Everly brothers, Pat Boone, the Flamingos, Larry Williams, Chuck Berry, Ray Charles, Bobby Darrin, Connie Francis… everybody that was hot. Alan Freed wanted to put us on that show and we couldn't believe it. This was going to be one of our big breaks

And that was in 1958. When I think about Romie, this is the reason why we split with him: We were getting ready to walk downtown to Brooklyn. It was so convenient, because the Fox Theatre was walking distance from our houses. Charles came to meet us. In the meantime, we were waiting for Romie to go with us to the gig. I'll never forget how it went down…

Romie was inside his apartment with his girlfriend, Lilly, and she said to him, "Listen, you say you love me, but you never prove it." Romie said, "What I got to do to prove it?" She told him, "Don't go to the Gig." He said, "I can't do that, you know how big this gig is." She responded, "Well if it's that important and you think I'm important, what's more important - your love for me or the gig?" And he said, "My love for you." So, he looked out the window and told us, "I'm not going to the gig."

Romie's father, Mr Ramos, was up at the window cursing in Spanish to his son, "You son of a bitch! You ain't going? You do that and I'll kill you!" But Romie was determined and it was getting late, so we had to go without him. So, the four of us - Charles Moffett, John Cheatdom, John Pearson, Donald Haywood - went down to the Fox Theatre. We were sitting there with all these big stars and we were going on after Bobby Darrin. *I think we were in about the sixth spot.* We said, "What are we going to do, we don't have a lead singer?" So, Donald said, "Look, I wrote the song. I'll sing it." And luckily, when we went out there, as soon as Donald said...*Can I come*... the girls started screaming and the rest is history. All they could hear was Donald singing the lead and Charles singing bass; and we got over successfully.

After that, we told Romie that he was done. Then we looked for a new lead singer and we had a lot of singers that came to audition. We selected Milton Love from the Southeast. He came to Brooklyn from Harlem to join the Velours; but he couldn't come back and forth because of neighbourhood gangs. We would always have to be traveling to Manhattan so Milton could rehearse with us. Milton eventually quit the group and started singing with the famous Harlem singing group, the Solitaires who had the hit song, "The Angels Sang."

Then we got a great singer, Keith Williams, from the Chesters, a group I had coached when Keith was a kid. We recruited him out of that group, and he sang with us for a while; but unfortunately, he got into trouble later and went to jail. We did, however, get to do some recordings with Keith, which was some great stuff. He sings *Blue Velvet* on one of the CDs.

TEN

FORMING THE FANTASTICS

To our surprise, when we first arrived in Britain in 1967, we discovered that we were to be billed as The Fabulous Temptations, and that we were expected to perform Motown songs. Despite the name change and the song line-up, we toured successfully. In 1968, we were invited to return, by Sheffield club owner Peter Stringfellow, this time under another new name.

Jerome Ramos, Don Haywoode and I had decided to reform our group. Actually, we formed a *new* group, adding tenor Richard Pitts; and then, we became the Fantastics. We were a very, very good group. We were four individual stars. Everybody was good! In fact, The Fantastics gained far greater success than we had ever achieved as the Velours.

The Fantastics remained in Britain, and recorded several singles released on MGM and then, later, on the Deram label in England. We then signed to Bell Records, and released "Something Old, Something New", a song written and produced by top British songwriters Tony Macaulay, Roger Greenaway, and Roger Cook. In 1971, the song rose to number nine on the UK singles chart, and reached number 102 in the US.

When we met Pete Stringfellow, he said to us, "One of these days, you guys are going to break up, you are too good to be together." And we just laughed it off. In 1967, we released the single "I'm Gonna Change" on MGM Records, and soon after, we agreed to undertake the tour in England. In 1968, after our first successful tour, we decided to move to the UK to take full advantage of the British Soul explosion!

When it comes to the world of nightclubbing, Stringfellow's is a household name. In 1986, Pete opened Stringfellow's – New York, which was successfully frequented by New York celebrities, rock stars and other personalities. In 1989, he opened Stringfellow's – Miami, and this was followed by Stringfellow's – Los Angeles in 1990.

For our group, being recognized by Pete Stringfellow was major. He is one of the most well-known nightclub owners in the world. In 1962, Stringfellow rented St. Aidan's Church Hall in Sheffield every Friday night, also known as the Black Cat Club. Several local bands played in the club, such as the Pursuers, Dave Berry and the Cruisers, Johnny Tempest and the Cadillacs; and from London - Screaming Lord Sutch, the Savages, Count Lindsay and Gene Vincent. Then Stringfellow's fortunes changed when the Beatles played on April 2,1963. The demand for concert tickets was so great that Stringfellow was forced to rent a larger venue, the Azena Ballroom in Sheffield.

In 1963, the now renowned Stringfellow began another club, the Blue Moon, at St. John's Church Hall in Sheffield. The opening act was the Marauders who had a record in the British top 30. More bands followed, such as the Kinks. Other bands that played at the club and who later became famous were Freddie Starr and the Midnighters, the Searchers, Shane Fenton and the Fentons, Wayne Fontana, Long John Baldry and the Hoochie Coochie Men, Rod Stewart and the Soul Agents, Vance Arnold & the Avengers, Dean Marshall and the Deputies. Also in the same year, Stringfellow's Theatre promotions at Sheffield City Hall were a big success. They featured acts such as the Rolling Stones, the Big Three, Fleetwood Mac and the Nice.

Still growing, in 1964, Stringfellow opened another club called King Mojo Club in Sheffield. During its three and half years of business, many bands played at the club, including the Who, Pink Floyd, Rod Stewart, Elton John and Jimi Hendrix. Besides our group, other American acts who played in the club, included the first Tamla/Motown acts to play in the UK, Ben E. King, Sonny Boy Williamson, Tina Turner and Little Stevie Wonder.

The Fantastics started getting booked by Pete Stringfellow at his Mojo Club, but he was getting into financial trouble there and he sold our contract to Howard Davidson, one of the world's most famous agents. Howard's first job was when he put us on tour with Diana Ross and the Supremes, their last tour together in Europe, which was amazing.

He called me up and said, "Look John, can you guys come down on the weekend?" We went down to London and signed our contracts and Howard Davidson became our agent. So, we got a tour with Diana Ross and the Supremes. We started going to the rehearsals and were scheduled to do four concerts - two shows at the London Palladium and two shows at the City of Manchester Stadium. So, we went and had a couple of new outfits made - beautiful purple and royal blue suits.

Howard said, "No problem, just go have them made; you know I want you guys looking good." So, we went down to rehearsal with the Supremes' Orchestra and when we got there the Musical Director, Jameson, was going over the Supremes' songs. He said to me, "John, are there any Supremes' songs that you guys sing?" We said, "Well yeah, but it doesn't matter, we'll sing something else." He said, "No…no what Supremes' songs do you do?" I responded, "We do 'Reflections' and we do 'Love Child'." He said, "Alright, take out 'Love Child' and let me replace it." *Are you serious?* He said, "We've got to play these songs." It was totally amazing, because most acts never ever would do anything like that.

We had two tours in the UK, with Frankie Valli and the Four Seasons. The first tour we did with Frankie Valli was a month long, at all the theatres in England. And the first thing Frankie did was to check on what our set list was and he said, "Well you can't sing this song, you can't sing that song…" I said, "Frankie that's all our big hits. Those are all the hits that we sing." He said, "Yeah, but I might sing it." *He knew he wasn't going to sing it*. But he just said, "I got the power and I say you ain't singing it." So, we just shut up because Frankie Valli was a big Mafia type. Just before we left England, the last thing that we did was to record a song with Bob Gardo, Franki Valli's partner in the Four Seasons.

It was a song called “I'm Going to Change”, which became a big hit over in England later on, in the northern soul circuit. We didn't even know it was such a big hit over here. Anyway, when we went to do our show, we said, “Listen we can't let him get away with that.” So, we went out to that show. We did Jackie Di Shannon’s “Put a Little Love in Your Heart” and “Oh Happy Day.” Bob Gardo went to the wings. He was pointing his fist at us, while we were on stage...and he shouted, “I'll bust your ass, your sons of a bitch! You’d bet get off that damn stage right now!”

And we said, “Oh my God!” So, we came off the stage and ran into the dressing room and he was banging on the door. “Open that damn door!!” We opened the door and Bob said, “Listen, let me tell you what the story is all about right now. You guys weren't going to sing those songs, but the thing about it is Frankie's just got this thing.” *Right.* Bob continued, “When we were working in Las Vegas, “You're Just Too Good to Be True,” was one of their hit records with Andy Williams. We sang with Andy Williams, opened up for him and then he told us, “I'm singing that song because you guys can't sing it.” Now can you imagine, we got one song and we can't sing it because Andy Williams said he wants to sing it because he's the star… and we had to go through that. That's why Frankie's got that thing on me, he's never forgotten about that. He didn't mean nothing by it, guys, so don't worry about it. Carry on. Everything will be fine.”

So, we did that tour with Frankie Valli and the Four Seasons once, and the second tour…I think it was a year later…or eighteen months later…

he asked us to do another one. Then we did another tour with them, which was really good and tight.

Okay, now getting back to the Supremes. The first show was in London, May 29, 1968 and it was the year that Martin Luther King, Jr. died. Diana Ross was doing a song that she dedicated to MLK. And she started talking and singing the song, and everybody was crying. I was crying and I thought, *that little girl can't make me cry.* I could not believe this girl, Diana Ross, has got something special about her that is amazing. *She got a little voice, but what she has done with her voice with a stage is just totally amazing. She is a true star.*

And we did four shows and we cried four times. But the most amazing thing about Diana Ross and the Supremes was so funny because we were in the dressing room and we were in there with Mary and Cindy. Diana would be coming in a minute, so the other girls were getting dressed, and at 6:21 the producer said, "Girls get dressed now." So, the announcer was still saying, "Well, Diana…" and suddenly, the music started playing. "…Ladies and Gentlemen, the Supremes!" and they came out of the dressing room and the back door was open. Diana Ross came out of a Limousine walked up the stairs, threw her fur coat out and said, "Hello girls, hello guys!" and she walked right on stage and did the show.

As soon as Diana finished, she said, "Goodnight!" Then she put her fur coat on, went right back out the door, and never spoke to the other girls at all. I mean, she just said hello and goodbye. What a performance! That was one of the highlights of my life, during those four days that we performed with Diana Ross. It was totally amazing… Diana was just a true star!

After we did that tour with Diana Ross and the Supremes, we broke really heavy into the scene in England. We started working all the big night clubs and then, like anything else, trouble started coming in. Guys started fighting, egos started coming out, and it was just horrible. Sometimes Romie had this ego that was totally unbearable. It just became very difficult to work with him, but unfortunately, he didn't just quit the group; instead he got busted for drugs.

Richie left because he and Donald couldn't get along anymore and he decided he was going to go solo. So, Richie launched a solo career, and we brought another guy in to replace him. We met the guy through the 5th Dimension, who we had done a concert with early that year. Billy Davidson had told us, "Anytime you guys need anyone for singles or something like that, call me." So, we called him and he sent a guy over named A.D. Beal, who was a tremendous singer.

He had just come out of the army and he joined us. A.D. put a whole new dimension on our show. Unfortunately, one night, after we had been working, A.D. and Romie had some young girls in the hotel and they were smoking some dope and stuff. Donald and I were asleep in our room. The police came, locked them up and all I know is they knocked on my door. When I opened it, I saw that A.D. and Romie had on handcuffs and I was in shock. I said, "I can't believe this. I came all the way over here and my career is going to end like this." I said, "I hope not." Howard Davidson tried everything to keep it out of the newspapers, and he did for four or five months. But then, finally, when they had to go to court, A.D. and Romie got deported. So, they left Donald and me in England… just the two of us.

After that incident, we recruited different guys, but it wasn't working. The Fantastics remained a popular live attraction in Britain for several years, though with several personnel changes. In 1972, the group's first single released on Decca's Deram Label was "The Best of Strangers Now" featuring a new first time lead singer, John Cheatdom.

Eddie Kendricks liked the song so much that he recorded it in his first solo LP. The Fantastics later recorded "(Love Me) Love the Life I Lead," written by Macaulay and Greenaway and produced by Greenaway. The song reached number 86 on the US *Billboard* pop chart, but it did not chart in Britain.

Richard Pitts' role in The Fantastics was part of a BBC Radio Four documentary by his son, the journalist and photographer, Johnny Pitts, entitled "Something Old Something New." The documentary was named after the Fantastics' hit record. Richard Pitts left in 1972, later becoming a lecturer at the University of Huddersfield, as well as working with another vocal group, The Invitations.

In 1976, The Fantastics decided to split up - both Ramos and I also left, leaving Donald Haywoode as the only original member and the then-owner of the group's name. By 1986, the Fantastics were still performing in Britain, on the nightclub and cabaret circuit, as a trio comprising Haywoode, and the newly recruited Elvin Hayes, and Emma St. John.

ELEVEN

ENTER THE REALISTICS

After The Fantastics split up, I formed another group called the Realistics. I recruited some old friends - some really good guys - all American guys who had also moved to the UK. We started touring as the Realistics and then we met an agent, named John Bannister from Chorley in Manchester. He said, "Hey you guys, we got some club dates for you in South Africa."

So, we went… and that was in 1976 during Apartheid in South Africa. We were playing for the Holiday Inn hotels owned by Rennes of London in Lesotho, Botswana and Swaziland. We toured through all those little African nations and it was interesting because we were working in several places and these countries didn't have Apartheid, but South Africa did. But when they asked us to go to work in South Africa we said we're not doing it. We said that we would work in the townships but we were not working in any place where there was segregation.

We did a couple of shows in some of the townships and we performed at some clubs in Durbin in the township. It was really good. We did that for a year, and then one of the guys in the group left. When Sandy left, we brought in a good friend of mine, who I'd been wanting to sing with for years - Jimmy Cherry from Miami, Florida. We called him

"Jazz" because of his dancing ability. He used to Limbo dance and go down really low to the floor. Jimmy was a really top singer and I recruited him into the group. We were together until just a couple of years ago.

Another great singer and perfect gentleman from Philadelphia, named Jimmy Hamilton, had been recommended to us by Richard Barrett. One of the most important figures in the 1950s and early-'60s rock & roll to come out of New York, Richard "Richie" Barrett has been badly served by history in terms of the recognition he is due. A singer/songwriter turned producer, Richie became an essential part of George Goldner's Rama, End, and Gone Records operations, as well as Morris Levy's Roulette Records. Richie brought along several legendary groups of the period, including: Frankie Lymon and the Teenagers, The Chantels and Little Anthony & the Imperials. He was also one of the first successful independent black record producers, having produced: The Isley Brothers, Harold Melvin & the Blue Notes, The Rap Machine and The Three Degrees, who he also managed. Richard Barrett was the guru of all the gurus.

Back in the day, Barrett used to nurture us when we were kids… when we first started in the music business as the Velours. We ran into Barrett one day, when we were going into the Brill Building at 1619 Broadway in New York City. The Brill Building was the place to be, the place where all aspiring and accomplished songwriters went to get their songs published and heard by notable recording artists and their managers. Donald and I met Richard Pitts there. Alan Lorber Music was paying the three of us $20 weekly for our time. He also gave us a room as an office. Donald, Richard and I were in the room next to Valerie Simpson's office before she hooked up with Ashford and formed Ashford & Simpson. Of the three of us, I was the only one to write a hit. In 1965, the hit female group The Toys recorded "My Love Sonata" which was a follow-up to their number 2 single "Lovers Concerto".

We had been fortunate to cross paths again with Richie Barrett, when he had taken a liking to our group, the Fantastics, which evolved into the Realistics. Upon Richie's recommendation, Jimmy Hamilton had joined the Fantastics in 1972 to replace Richard Pitts. Richie and Jimmy were both wonderful guys. We were like brothers and had a really good and long-lasting friendship. Sadly, Richie Barrett passed away in 2000.

A few years after the first tour, the Realistics had an opportunity to return to South Africa. Booking agent, Ian McDonald, asked us to go to Sun City to perform on a show with Gloria Gaynor and that was a tremendous 10 days. We really did a great show. There were just three of us – Jimmy Hamilton, Jimmy (Jazz) Cherry and me - and we were probably one of the best groups in Europe or in the world at the time. We were really, really hot. It was just totally amazing.

When we left Sun City the promoters asked us if we would put together a tour for the whole of South Africa; so, we assembled an 8-piece band, from the four Afican tribes and toured South African for 6 months.

We started up in Durbin on the East coast and went straight around to the Cape. This was 1980 and the tour was very, very successful. The strange thing about working in South Africa during Apartheid was different than segregation in America, because in America we knew where to go, we knew what to do and what not to do. But over in South Africa, if you were an American you could go any place you wanted to go. Just in case, whenever we had members of our band, if we went somewhere we took them so that they could get into the place.

For instance, if we went to a shop they could go in that shop with us, but they couldn't go into the shop by themselves… so we got used to that kind of situation. But the thing about it was we never got black-balled like Ray Charles and all the other singers did, because we worked in the township first and we learned about how the people handled the situation. We heard a lot of chatter in South Africa, especially when we went downtown.

We used to go visit the children in mental homes. But, it was so hurtful because you got the coloureds, you got the blacks, you got the Indians, you got the whites and they all had their own different mental homes. An Indian child doesn't know that he's got the same illness as the black kids. They know they're all the same, they're all ill, but they put the kids in separate homes. So anytime we had to go do something, we always had to do the same things three or four different times. It was painstaking, but it was rewarding and we didn't mind. We used to do it because we thought it was a great opportunity.

There was one thing that really struck us in a disheartening way about the people in South Africa… the "coloureds" thought they were white. They didn't know that in America they would be considered black.

When we used to have parties and other events, we would invite coloured - light skin girls - to a party and they were walking in and they would see African - dark skin girls. They said, "We can't go in there because some Africans are in there." I told them, "Listen you're all the same, you're all black." They always responded, "No we ain't black." I said, "What colour am I then?" They said, "You're American." I said, "I'm the same colour you are. Where I come from, I'm black so you got to get used to the fact that you're black." They didn't want to hear that. I thought, *well sooner or later they'll get the message.* It was a very enlightening experience working in South Africa.

The Realistics toured extensively. We worked all the club circuits in several different locations including: India, Dubai, Sajida, and we even did Emirates. We recorded a song called "Pure Magic" which was a big hit in that part of the world and we were also featured on television, performing "Pure Magic". I was hoping it would not be my last time performing over there. *I didn't know it at the time, but I would return to South Africa again in later years with the Platters.*

When we went back to London after we did that six-months' tour, we were asked to be part of a TV series on Channel 5- a new channel that was just started. The Producer, Johnny Worth, called me up and he asked me if I would sing the theme song, "Crazy Music." I said, "By myself?" He said, "Yeah." So, I went in and I recorded "Crazy Music" and our group did this TV series for three years on Channel 5. That was tremendous. We had singles performed by the Stylistics, or one of those groups. It was really a good show, we had a wonderful time.

TWELVE

MEETING RONA

It was on a cold Saturday evening in February 1970. My group, the Fantastics, had a night off and I decided to go down to my favourite soul club, the Q club to spend some time with my friend, the owner, Count Suckle; and to listen to the latest hit songs from America played by the great disc jockey, Steve Bernard. As I walked into Q Club, I noticed a group of ladies sitting by the door. I waved and said, "Hello." Then, I noticed a young lady there that I had not seen before. I ask Steve if he knew who the lady was that I pointed out to him and he said, "Yes, her name is Rona."

The next time I saw her, it was four months later at the military club called the Douglas House in London, which was managed by Smithy, who was a friend of mine from Brooklyn. I ask him if that lady over the other side of the club with her friends was named Rona and he said, "Yes." He took a drink to her table and said it was from his friend standing at the bar and she acknowledged me, *what a wonderful smile*.

Later in the evening, I asked Smithy what she said to him; and he replied she said, "Who is your fat friend?" I was devastated. I was 5 feet 8 inches tall, weighed 210 pounds (15 stones), with a 37-inch waist and a 16 ½ inch neck. Now in America, that's not fat; but I guess in London, it is. So, I was determined to lose weight. I purchase an isometric wheel and started exercising, and eating and drinking less.

I went on a European tour with the Fantastics for five months and by the time I returned to London I had lost 56 pounds (4 stones). I went back to the Q club and when I saw one of Rona's friends, I inquired about her. Before the end of the evening, Rona's friend came back with her phone number (She must have told her I had lost weight). It took me two weeks to get up the courage to call Rona. But, when I eventually called her, I invited her to dinner. She preferred to have lunch with me, rather than dinner and asked me to meet her at lunchtime.

I met her at an Indian restaurant, situated in downtown London. Then I found out that she was 19 years old, born in Jamaica but raised in London, and her real name was Hyacinth. For someone so young, she had a great job working for the Rank Film Organization. Rona and her India colleague, Nadia, used to fly to all the film festivals around Europe choosing films for Ranks Odeon Cinemas (Movie Houses) in the UK.

Our romance flourished. In 1976, I left the Fantastics to form a new group called the Realistics. That same year, the Rank Organisation decided to bring the Jacksons to England. Rona recommended the Realistics as the opening act and that really helped to promote our group. We did not have a backing band, at the time. as I was just in the process of putting the group together. So I borrowed the backing band from my good friend Chris Amoo's group called The Real Thing. The show was a success.

Rona and I got married in London in 1982. We have two great Sons, John Junior and Blake.

THIRTEEN

BACK IN LONDON

One of the best things about the whole South African experience occurred a couple of years after I had returned to London. I was at home relaxing in between shows, and I received a call from an old friend. Rona answered the phone and said, "Hello. Who is this?"

He answered, "My name is Pejeta."

Then I picked up the phone and asked, "Who is this? It's Mr. John Cheatdom, who is this? Pejeta?" Then I said, "How you doing?"

He responded, "Alright."

I said, "Where are you?"

"I'm in London", he replied.

I said, "What are you doing in London?"

He said, "Oh we went for assignment with the Graceland Band."

I said to myself, *That's the band that we put together, the first time we went to South Africa.*

Then Pejeta told me, "We recorded the hit LP "Graceland," produced by Paul Simon from New York and we took the band out of South Africa."

Paul was the other half of Simon & Garfunkle, the internationally successful duo. Paul wrote and produced the entire CD, which sold millions around the world. Paul had heard about this great band in South Africa, the band that I had personally assembled, and used them for all the Simon & Garfunkle LPs. The band was paid record royalties and became very rich; they toured with Paul Simon around the world for many years. They were great guys.

When I heard that they were with Paul Simon, I just folded my hands and cried like a baby. I just couldn't believe that they were able to make it…*they were so good.* We couldn't get them out of South Africa. But if we had gotten them out of South Africa then, they wouldn't have had the success that they are having with Paul Simon, because of the international popularity of some of the guys that work with them now. We were able to get those local guys, put a band together and they had experienced major success. I was ecstatic, even though we didn't make any money out of it; but just due to the fact of knowing that we put those guys together and they stayed together long enough to be discovered. It was so gratifying.

JOHN CHEATDOM'S PHOTO MEMORIES MAKING MUSIC ON THE ROAD

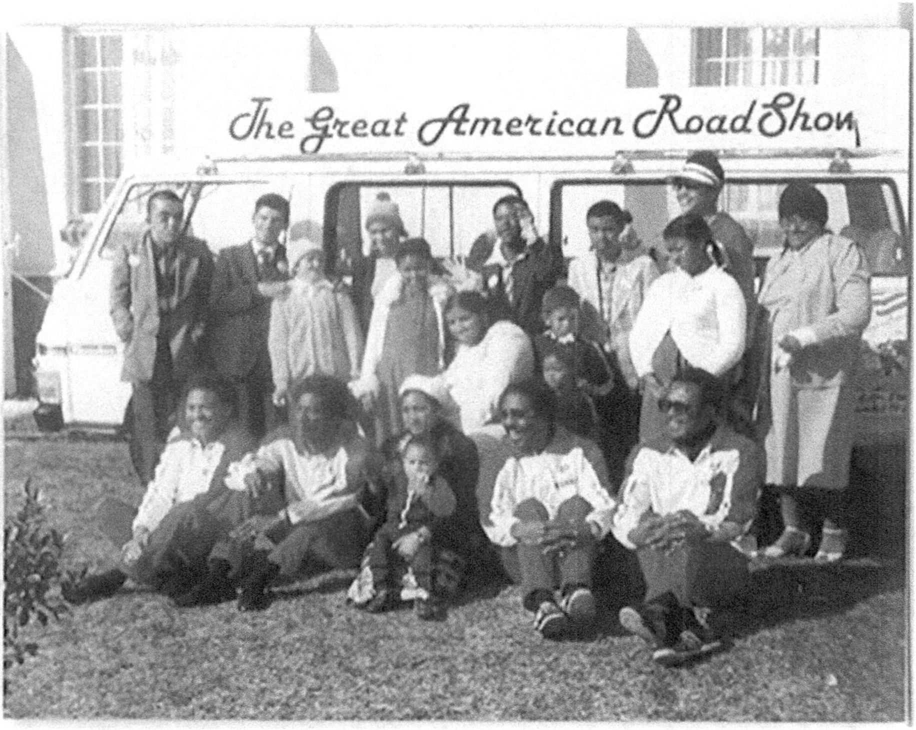
The Great American Road Show

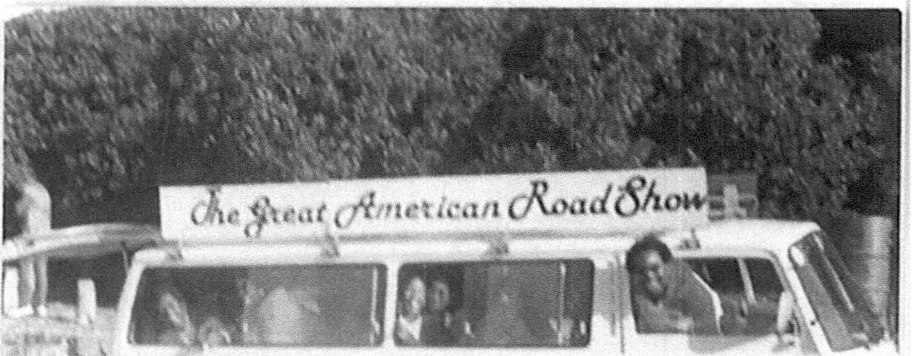
The Great American Road Show

Drum's Red Devils bite the dust

BY KERRY "MAD MLUNGU" SWIFT. PICTURES BY CHESTER "HOT LENS" MAHARAJ.

It's celebrity soccer as Drum plays Capital

[B]EFORE 25 000 delirious fans, DRUM's 'Red Devils' took the field at Orlando Stadium for their debut match against Capital Radio.

Despite their massive weight advantage, 22 left feet, three American musical superstars (who had never seen a football before), our own Richard Jon Smith and a few extra players, the 'Red Devils' saw victory slip past their fumbling feet by two goals to one.

"It was a fix," said the 13 exhausted DRUM players at the end of the match — and instantly challenged the winners to a replay. They were referring to a first-half incident when the opposition claimed Richard Jon Smith had picked up the ball and tried to take it home to his kids.

The ref, who refused to be named for fear of reprisals, had earlier been given a Capital Radio T-shirt. Needless to say, he blew for a penalty.

DRUM'S goalkeeper, 'Mad Mlungu' made a valiant attempt to keep the shot out by throwing his boots at the ball but, alas, Capital's Mark Greenstein scored with a rebound off 'Mad Mlungu's' glasses.

The Realistics, John, Jazz and Jimmy had this to say: "Hey man, w-h-a-a-t a rip-off. Give us grid-iron football any-day," at which point Jimmy left the field and was replaced by a couple of sympathetic professionals from the previous game.

In the second half, DRUM's Meshack Dlamini, who claimed to be a former Swallows star, hammered home a glorious equaliser.

Then, much against the run of play, and from an obviously off-side position, Capital Radio scored the winner which whistled through 'Mad Mlungu's' legs.

It was all over bar the drinking. The best team lost, but they made up for it later in Jimmy's tavern at the Bosmont Hotel where the Realistics sang ballads in three-part harmony while the 'Red Devils' drowned their sorrows.

DRUM would like to thank Ismael Pahad, boss of Dynamos and George Thabe of SANFA for allowing us to play at Orlando. Watch out for more exploits from DRUM F.C. in the future.

If you think your team is as bad as ours, give us a call — we've got to win sometime.

1. DRUM's centre-forward, Richard Jon Smith kicks and misses as the men from Capital Radio watch transfixed.

2. OUR celebrity guests at Orlando, Richard Jon and those ever-nice fellas, Jimmy, John and Jazz who make up The Realistics. Unfortunately for the Red Devils, these superstars are not so hot at soccer as they are on the stage. Still, DRUM's staff ain't much better, either!

3. DRUM F.C. fall about for a team photo before the game. They were still falling about after the opening whistle blew.

44 DRUM December 1980

LIBERTY
CAR-HIRE

JAZZ
JOHN
JIMMY
1980 AFRICAN TOUR
THE Realistics
I.A.P.
COUNT
PUSHKIN
the world's
best vodka

FOURTEEN

TOURING THE WORLD

The call from Pejeta regarding the success of the Graceland Band was one of the real highlights of my life. That's just one of them, there are so many, but here's another one.

In 1981, after we did the "Unforgettable" TV series, the Realistics had split up and I got a phone call from Ernie Wright, who was in Little Anthony and the Imperials. I had been their vocal coach when they were kids living in the projects near where I was born.

In 1957, a doo-wop group known as the Chesters was founded with a group of young guys from New York. One of the original members, Ronald Ross, dropped out of the Group and was replaced by Ernest Wright. The group recorded briefly for Apollo Records, but then were picked up by End Records, at which point they changed their name to the Imperials. Their first single was "Tears on My Pillow", which was an instant hit. It sold over one million copies, and was awarded a gold disc by the RIAA. (While playing their song, D.J. Alan Freed came up with the name "Little Anthony".) The B-side, "Two People in the World", was also a hit. The group followed up with "Shimmy, Shimmy, Ko Ko Bop" in 1960. Their success started to dwindle, and ultimately Wright left in 1971 to join Tony Williams' Platters.

So, in 1981 my old friend Ernie Wright called me and said, "We're in Germany. If you're not busy, do you want to come and join us because one of the guys left?" I wasn't touring at the time, I was performing locally, doing a couple of solo gigs in London. So, I said, "Okay." I went to Germany and met Ernie and the guys… they were doing a Platter's tour. They were not the "original" Platters; but, nonetheless, they called themselves the Platters. I said, "Oh you're the "Magic Platters", okay!

We toured all over Germany, Austria and Switzerland. It was fantastic, what a wonderful tour that was! They asked me if I would stay with the group and I really wasn't doing much of anything. So, I said, "Swell! And, of course, those guys were like my little brothers, anyway. We were all like family.

After I said okay, I stayed on with the group and then the girl who was singing with them fell in love with the drummer, Audi. She quit and then moved to Switzerland, so we were looking for a female singer and a friend of mine in London told me that he heard this girl, named Jackie Benjamin, sing. She was young, but he said she was good. So, I called her, and she came out to my house and auditioned. Even though Jackie was only 19 she was a great singer, so we put her in the group. When Jackie left to get married, Ernie was still in the group. He didn't leave the Platters until after she got married.

When Ernie left, I stayed with the group, and recruited another female named Patrice Murray. She was a very good singer from Trinidad. She was actually a solo artist working in London. Her brother is Sir Derek Murray, the great Cricketer from Trinidad. At the time, Patrice Murray was in a band called the Light of the World, which was like one of those 70s Love, Rock, Jazz type bands. Patrice was their lead singer.

When I met Patrice, I was really interested in the Light of the World's Congo player. He was very good and I had previously heard him perform in the club. Somebody told me about him and I went down to see him and he said that he would like to join us. But the thing about it was, he never liked our kind of music - the Platters' music. He was more of a modern-time singer. So instead, I recruited Patrice.

Ernie Wright had left the Platters to go solo. But, when Ernie was approached by Dick Clark to go back to America to reform little Anthony and the imperials, he left us on the spot and we had to revamp. Ernie was replaced by a guy I had met, who was in London, in the club circuit. Milton Brown, a school teacher from Norfolk, Virginia, stayed with the group for three years. During that time, we worked and toured in Israel, visiting all the major cities.

Milton and his wife Deborah were both singers, in another group. After Milton joined us, he had a lot of problems when we were traveling back and forth between countries. Every week, we went from England to Belgium to Holland. He kept asking, "Why? What are you doing this week and that week?" Because we travelled so much, he was worried about his teaching license and the fact that he might get thrown out of England, if the authorities started inquiring about it too much. Anyway, at the end of the year, that was why Milton decided to leave the group.

That's when we got Gene Bello from one of the clubs we used to hang out in. Gene stayed with us for two years and, during that time, we got invited to tour in South Africa. The fact was I had a lot of friends in South Africa, whom I had met when I was down there with the Realistics. When people found out that I was now in the Platters, they invited us down in 1994 for the Year's Photo. Then we got an offer from a supermarket chain, called Pick and Pay, to promote their stores and to record an album for them. Gene was an excellent producer and songwriter, so we went down to Johannesburg. And, we produced an album of songs that were all written by Gene except for a few Platters songs that we put in. The album was called the "Magic Sound of the Platters Full Circle." But, unfortunately, it was only recorded and not released for that particular event.

We toured the country for a month. We sold the albums and a lot of CDs. It was a very successful time in South Africa, because the country was getting together and black people and white people were going to clubs and concerts together. It was really nice to see and we were glad that we could be part of that whole change-over. It was another one of the highlights of my life, the fact that we could be a part of that whole transition. It was really tremendous.

After we returned from South Africa, Gene decided he wanted to go solo. Then, after Gene left, we ran into a singer in Germany who worked on the club circuit as a solo artist. His name was Tommy Smiley. He was an R&B Blues singer, who used to do a Platters show. (During that time, I think there were about five different "Platters" groups touring internationally). We asked Tommy to join us and he said he would for a while, to see how it would turn out. It was during the same time that we recruited Patrice Murray.

Tommy had been working with the Platters, when they broke up five years prior. He had toured with the Platters in Argentina and places like that. When Tommy joined our group, he had some contacts in Argentina that he had worked with previously. Tommy had a girlfriend in Argentina. He had gone down to South America with a different group of Platters and they became very established there. One of the performers in the group had been Paul Robby. Paul died, so they recruited Tommy and he was working there with them for years. Then the Platters broke up, and the group left Argentina. I didn't actually know that until we met Tommy and he said he'd been singing with the Platters for years; but he wanted to do more solo work in Germany because he was more comfortable there. It turned out that he lived in Germany and his girlfriend had a night club there, so he was pretty comfortable moving on.

Anyway, when we asked Tommy if he would join us for a while, he did. We had a great working relationship. Then, Tommy had an idea to call one of his friends in Argentina to see if there was still work down there. He called Barry Smith, who he had been there for 20 years, and he asked him if they were still working there. And Barry said, "Ya, but the guys aren't very good, they are all drugged out." Then Tommy said, well I've got these singers here - John Cheatdom and Patrice Murray.

Patrice had joined us, so that was the new group - Tommy Smiley, Patrice Murray and me. I had met Patrice in London. She was there from Trinidad and Tobago, studying for her master's degree. When I met her, she told me, "Look, if I join the group, maybe I can do some traveling and write a book or something." *But, after a year, she put the book down*. Patrice, Tommy and I went down to Argentina. We started working in Argentina and also traveled back and forth to Mexico, Uruguay, Paraguay and Chile. It was fantastic.

But, keeping a group together was not easy. Patrice joined us right after we had recorded our album "The Platters Sing Mariachi' in Mexico." After being with us for a few years, Patrice decided she wanted to leave and go back to Belgium to be with her boyfriend and get married. He owned a nightclub there.

It ended up that I worked in Argentina and Mexico for almost a total of 10 years. Sometimes, though, it was a bit rough because we had so many problems with all these drug cartels. We would go to some places and they would be shooting up people and it would be quite dangerous, especially in Mexico.

We were lucky that someone knew a female singer from Atlanta, Georgia. Her name was Marilyn Blackburn. She came over and joined us in 2004 after Patrice left the group. Soon after Marilyn joined the group, we were approached by a tequila company owner to make an album with the Mariachi Orchestra. So, we went in the studio in Mexico City and recorded the album, called "The Platters Sing Mariachi" with them. Mariachi music is the sound of Mexico. It is the musical accompaniment to the important moments in life. A Mariachi band is a Mexican musical group consisting of four or more musicians that wear *charro* suits. A Charro costume is the typical dress of a Mexican horseman. Mariachi is popular throughout Mexico and the Southwest United States, and is considered representative of Mexican music and culture.

When we were in Mexico City, we would always see groups of Mariachi singers in the streets. Or in Mexican restaurants, they walk around singing, going from table to table. They have a special blend of music that's recognizable throughout the world. We recorded the album, half in Cancun and half in Mexico City and when it came out there was instant success. We were working at clubs and in theatres in Mexico, and at Mexican venues throughout California, Texas and New Mexico.

In 2004, I had a rheumatoid arthritis attack. It was so painful because rheumatoid arthritis attacks both sides - arms, elbows, knees, legs and hips. I was working in Spain with the Platters when I had the attack. The pain was excruciating. My whole body swelled up. The guys in the group rushed me to the hospital.

The doctor told me I had rheumatoid arthritis. So, he gave me some medicine and told me I've got to go home to London straightaway. I said, "Listen, I'm not going anywhere. I am not gonna quit working and I am not going back to London." I said, "I've got a gig." We used to work in Spain every year from September to November. We would play one or two gigs in a week in different cities.

We had an apartment in Valencia. I would lay in bed all week. Barry Smith and Fred Lyons cooked for me and made sure I was okay in the flat, but I couldn't move. Every time I moved, everything ached. I must have cried every day for three years. The pain was terrible, so when the weekend came and it was time for me to do the show, they would pick me up. And when it was time for me to do the show there would be people in the audience who knew me for years. I used to walk around the stage and sing and I was singing the same songs, but people were saying "What's wrong with John? How come he's not moving around?"

I was screaming, "Ahh! Ahh!" And the guys called my wife and told her she had to come get me. I told her, "Don't you come get me! I'll have to listen to you!" I ended up going back home to London and I went to the hometown hospital. I told the doctor that I had been referred from Valencia Hospital in Spain. The doctor looked at me and said, "Inflammatory Rheumatism." He prescribed Methotrexate, one of the strongest medications I can take.

Methotrexate is used to treat certain types of cancer of the breast, skin, head and neck, or lung. It is also used to treat severe psoriasis and rheumatoid arthritis. Methotrexate is often prescribed after other medications have been tried without successful treatment of symptoms. Methotrexate is usually taken once or twice per week and not every day. You must use the correct dose for your condition. Some people have died after taking methotrexate every day by accident.

After a year, the pain went away and I was able to walk comfortably again. The pain had been so bad I was walking with a cane and I was looking older than I look now - I was looking like an *old man.* I am fine now, and the fact is, I was just lucky that I lived in England because we didn't have to pay for medications or anything. Aside from my Inflammatory Rheumatism, Mexico had been a great experience.

The good times lasted up until 2012, when Tommy had a heart attack and died. What was most horrible about that, was the night he died we had done a concert and a TV show. And, when we went back to the hotel, Tommy said that he was thinking of turning his life over, living a cleaner life, because he took a lot of drugs.

But sadly, that night, Tommy died. When I went into his room, he was sitting on the toilet seat with no clothes on - dead. Barry and I took him off the toilet seat and laid him on the floor. Then Barry left to call the police and I was in the room trying to resuscitate him, but to no avail. He kept getting colder and colder. When the police and the coroner came, they took me down to the hospital. Then they asked me, "Did he have a heart attack or did he die from a drug overdose?"

It was really terrible the way they treated me. I was at the hospital for eight hours, and all over the TV, there were pictures of our group, and the newscasters were saying that Tommy had died. They called us Las Plateras in Argentina and in Mexico they called us Las Plaza – we were very popular and the people mourned Tommy. I got very disillusioned and I went back home to London. When I got home, I would just sit around the house and I didn't work for about six or seven months.

Then I got a call from a guy I had met years ago – his name was Nino Cathi, Junior. I had met him when I first came to England. He said, "If you're not doing anything I want you to come join my crew," and I told him that I would consider it. I started working with Nino and it was easy because I already knew the Drifters and all the songs from Motown.

Then he talked me into reviving the Platters again, so I called Jackie to see how she was doing because I hadn't seen her in years. She said, "I raised three kids, now I'm ready to get back to singing." We got a new male singer, named Lamar, who had been in the Drifters. He was laying around doing nothing, at the time. So, Lamar joined us and we started doing concerts and other events. But, then he returned home to Canada and we ended up with yet another singer.

He was a very young guy named Wayne Copley. Wayne was a great singer. He stayed with us for about three years. Then he decided to go solo, but when Bruno Mars exploded onto the music scene, Lamar joined him instead. After Wayne, we got Alan Cooper. He was really, really good and we were glad to have him join the group. So, we just keep moving on.

As long as my voice is holding up and my legs can hold up, and I can step out on the stage, I'll just keep performing until I drop. I have loved to perform ever since I started singing, as a young kid, in the church choir. I admit that I'm not in love with performing as much as I was when I first started. But what else can I do? It's my life. I just love singing to people, seeing smiling faces, and all that comes with the entertainment business.

FIFTEEN

WRAPPING UP

In ***Keeping Doo-Wop Alive: One Man's Story of Strength, Stamina & Survival as an International Entertaine***r, I have thoroughly enjoyed recalling my journey through life. I have shared with you everything that I've been told and all that I can recall starting from the day of my birth and including the history of my mother and other family members that I was blessed to know and spend time with as a child.

I have told you about my first 64 years in show business, including the trials and tribulations, the ups and downs; and through it all, I have battled with crippling arthritis and almost career-ending throat problems from 2004-2010.

The story of John Cheatdom, international entertainer, actually begins when I was sixteen years old, shaping my future while embarking upon a career as a professional singer in the entertainment industry. It is a story about a young singer who lived through the horrors that began in the '50s and spans more than six decades right up to the present day.

Throughout my journey, but I always showed up because as an international entertainer, it has been my job and my pleasure to spread joy to every audience that I encountered. I witnessed many horrific events happening in the world, including: Segregation in the 50s and 60s in America's South; Apartheid in South Africa in the late 70s and 80s; and Drug Wars and corruption in North, Central and South America from 1999 – 2006.

The 1950s and 1960s Civil Rights Movement in the United States achieved the passage of several significant pieces of federal legislation to overturn discriminatory practices. From 1964 through 1970, a wave of inner city riots in black communities undercut support from the white community. I was twenty-six years old and living in Brooklyn, New York when the Harlem riot of 1964 occurred between July 16 and 22, 1964. It began after James Powell was shot and killed by police Lieutenant Thomas Gilligan. The second bullet of three fired by Lieutenant Gilligan killed the 15-year-old African American in front of his friends and about a dozen other witnesses. Immediately after the shooting, about 300 students from a nearby school, who were informed by the principal, rallied. The shooting set off six consecutive nights of rioting that affected the New York City neighbourhoods of Harlem and Bedford-Stuyvesant.

In total, 4,000 New Yorkers participated in the riots which led to attacks on the New York City Police Department, vandalism, and looting in stores. At the end of the conflict, reports counted one dead rioter, 118 injured, and 465 arrested. It is said that the Harlem race riot of 1964 is the precipitating event for riots in July and August in cities such as Philadelphia, Pennsylvania; Rochester, New York; Chicago, Illinois; Jersey City, New Jersey; Paterson, New Jersey; and Elizabeth, New Jersey.

The emergence of the Black Power movement, which lasted from about 1966 to 1975, challenged the established black leadership for its cooperative attitude and its practice of nonviolence, instead, demanding political and economic self-sufficiency to be built in the black community. Throughout the years, it has always been the same story with rioting which is triggered by racism when the police target Blacks, most of whom are innocent victims. The retaliation is brutal and often deadly with beatings, shootings, lives lost, businesses destroyed – burned or bombed and unjustified arrests.

By this time, I was living in the U.K. But, of course, the riots are not only happening in the United States, they are everywhere. Because I am an entertainer and have spent most of my life touring, I have witnessed similar tragedies throughout the world. While touring, there were dangers all around me, stemming from racism, drugs, bombings and religious differences. I toured South Africa in the 70s and 80s, but still persevered in order to entertain the people for 10 years during the frightening aspects of apartheid.

While my band and I were touring in South Africa, the Soweto uprising occurred. There was a series of protests led by black school children in South Africa that began on the morning of June 16, 1976. Students from numerous Sowetan schools began to protest in the streets of Soweto in response to the introduction of Afrikaans as the medium of instruction in local schools. It is estimated that 20,000 students took part in the protests. They were met with fierce police brutality. The number of protesters killed by police is usually given as 176, but estimates of up to 700 have been made. In remembrance of these events, the 16th of June is now a public holiday in South Africa, named Youth Day.

Later I worked in Mexico under the backdrop of the dangerous drug cartels. One time when we were performing the bullets started to fly.

Then there was Belfast Ireland, amidst the bombings that occurred because of the religious war.

Things were rolling quite well; but then when the (911) September 11, 2001 Terrorist attacks occurred in the United States, everything fell apart because the first thing that happens when there's an international tragedy or disaster is the entertainers suffer and all entertainment stops. All our corporate work in Europe just disappeared. The venues stopped hiring the big acts. They just started using karaoke and discos, so we were really stuck for something to do.

Finally, things were looking up. We started touring Germany again and then we met a racing driver Dew Fenny, and he asked us if we would go into studio and do a Platters album. We said, "Well, we can't do a "Platters" album. He said, "I got permission to do it." We said, "Okay." So then, we went in and recorded all the Platters' songs again and that album was called "The Come Back." When we started the album, it was cold in Brussels, so while we were recording it, he took us to California. It turned out to be a wonderful album. We told him he could release it over in Europe, but my group wasn't required to go back to Brussels anymore. They could just stay in Las Vegas, United States and when the album came out we sold 3 million copies … it went straight into the charts. It was wonderful.

"The Magic Sound of the Platters… The Come Back" album was really great. We stayed together another few years until Ernie got an offer to go solo and he left the group. *Years later, in 1992 Ernie reunited with some of the former members of the Imperials under a new name but subsequently began touring with the renamed group - Little Anthony & the Imperials - again.*

I am still touring with the Magic Sound of The Platters. There are four of us now…Alan Cooper, Dino Cassar, Debbie and me. However, our current group - the Platters - work all over England and throughout Europe and Africa, whenever and wherever we are booked. Our audiences are great supporters and show us lots of love, with standing ovations, whenever we perform our hit songs.

From time to time, I have health issues bur after all, I am now 79 years old. *I am the last surviving member of the "original" Velours.*

If my music business career ended now, I wouldn't have any regrets because I really enjoyed myself. We recorded on several record labels, including: MGM, Deran and Bell, Onyx, CBS, Continental Records, The Bronze Label, The End Label, BMG, Beram, Papagei, Surf Records and we charted on *Billboard* several times.

Through the years, I established a wonderful relationship that I have with Gladys Knight and the Pips. I first met them in Detroit, in 1960. The Velours were doing a show there with the disk jockey, Mickey. It was supposed to be one of the biggest Rock and Roll shows ever. We were with Fats Domino, The Schoolboys, Lee Anderson and The Hearts - a whole big array of stars. Anyway, the show, for some reason didn't attract many fans and it folded after four days. So, we were stranded in Detroit.

We called the union – American Federation of Radio and Television Artists (AFTRA) and they said, "Listen, there's a gig this weekend." This was Wednesday and they told us there was a gig on Saturday. Then they said, "We'll send you enough money to get there to do the gig." The funniest thing about this whole incident was this happened when we were in the height of our career.

Anyway, the second night we were in our show at the theatre, we got a knock on the door and there were four kids standing there, actually five of them, as a matter of fact. They said, "Hello, we are the Pips." And I said, "Hello, how are you doing?" They said, "Boy, you guys are really good. We hope one day we are big stars like you guys." I think it must have been six or seven months later, when we heard "Giving up," which was their first release. No, "Every Beat of My Heart", was the first song by the Pips. And I said, "Listen to that, I can't believe it."

With me moving to England, I didn't see The Pips until they started coming over to England on the Motown tour, and then of course when they started getting these big hit songs like, "Help Us Through the Night," and we started hanging out with them. Sometimes they used to stay at the Savoy Hotel. Edward used to call me and say, "John, I'm coming over there to hang out. I can't stay in this hotel." Or, he would come over to where I live now, at Black Plaza. And he would have his limousine parked outside and people used to wonder, *who is that over there with John*?

It was Edward, from the Pips. He used to come stay with me. And then, sometimes Gladys would come over for a drink or something like that. She and my wife became relatively close. We also used to go over to their hotel for dinner - it had to be 1974 or 1975.

The Pips used to come to London to do the Royal Command Performance for the Queen. Rona and I went to their concerts at the Palladium to see them perform, they were sensational. Then after the concert, we used to go back to the hotel with them. They loved to party. So, one time, on the way to their hotel, Rona said, "Listen John, stop and get a bottle." I said, "For what?" She said, "You know, you're going to the hotel with all these stars there, at least you can take a drink." And, of course, I said like most people would say, "They have all the drinks there in the world." She said, "That's not the point! You stop and get a bottle!" So, we stopped the cab and got a bottle of cognac and took it to the hotel. And, when we got to the hotel and knocked on the door - it was a suite - Gladys' brother opened the door and he said, "Hey everybody! John Cheatdom and his wife, Rona, are here." I handed him the bottle. The place was packed with celebrities and he said, "Hey, listen up! I'm standing here with a bottle of cognac in my hand that John and Rona just gave me. This is the first time that anyone ever brought anything to a party and has given us anything that we've had. I'm so happy about this and I'm gonna tell you one thing: I'm drinking this. Ain't none of you all getting any of this!"

Gladys Knight and the Pips were great people. I remember when my son John was born - his name is also john Cheatdom. He was born 7/7/77 - we have the same birthday. His nickname is Jamie. When he was born, Gladys used to tell us to bring Jamie over to the hotel. So, I would bring him over there and she decided that she wanted to take Jamie on tour. Gladys was very fond of Jamie and she asked me and my wife if she and Edward could be Jamie's godparents. We told her that we would be delighted. She said, "We will be coming back to London soon, don't have the christening until then."

Well, unfortunately they never came back after they returned home to the United States. Gladys left the group, soon after, and I never saw her anymore until she came back and did a solo concert about 7 years ago at Royal Albert Hall. She sent us some tickets to go see the show and they said, "After the show, come backstage and see us." When we arrived at the concert, we had great seats and that was the first time I had seen Gladys on stage without the Pips. Now it was Gladys by herself, with her brother, Bubba, who is her road manager. Bubba comes out on the stage with Gladys and they do all the steps that they did, with all the songs from the Pips.

I was sitting there watching them do the songs – "Friendship Train" and the others - and I just broke out crying. Rona said, "John, come on." But, I just kept bawling and bawling and she got up and said, "Let's go! I'm not staying here with that." So, we left. We got a cab and went home. I never got to see Gladys that night and regrettably, I haven't seen her since then.

I am "Still Standing." I continue to perform because I say, "I can't let these people down. I have to get out there and do those shows." The thing is, show business becomes a part of you.

After battling Rheumatoid Arthritis and undergoing two operations on my throat, I am fine. Recently, I had two knots growing in my throat, and a surgeon had to remove them. My voice was back after four or five months, just as strong as ever - maybe even stronger than back when I first arrived in London. So, my voice is fine, my legs are fine and I am happy, as long as I can keep doing this. But, one day, I won't be able to do it. Right now, I am fine.

When I was 19 years old and my mother asked me how much money I was making. I wasn't making much at the time, just income from touring. So, I asked my mother if she knew how many girls I had. A lot has changed since then so, I think my mother would be very proud of me now.

My career in Entertainment has been very rewarding. In addition to my income from touring, I also have income from publishing. I wrote two songs for the Platters, "Near you" and "Champagne," and I am signed with a European publishing company called Savam Society of Music at Luxemburg.

I have made quite a bit of money from my songs. We bought the place we live in here in London, we bought a house in Jamaica and we had a house in Mexico City where I lived with the Platters for ten years.

I have no complaints…it's been great! With the shows I have committed to now, I can say that I am *almost* retired. Whenever I choose too, I can just sit back and relax and enjoy myself with my family.

SPECIAL ACKNOWLEDGEMENTS

The time we spent with Gladys Knight and the Pips through the years, was something really special, because they were special people. While I am reminiscing, I can't help but think about all those people that I have met and performed with through the years. I'd like to give ***special acknowledgements to some very special people.***

From the time they started their entertainment careers, showbusiness never affected them. They did not let their fame affect them in a negative way, and they just never ever changed, starting with Gladys Knight and the Pips.

I'd also like to give special mention to the Four Tops - Levi, Larry, Duke and Obi. People thought Obi and I were brothers, we looked just alike. In fact, there were three people who looked alike in show business - me, Obi from the Four Tops and the old rock and roll-blues singer, Larry Williams. We all looked just like brothers, and to top it off, they were both really great people.

I met people like Harold Melvin and the Blue Notes when they came to London; but they were from Philadelphia and they were like a different kind of breed than the New York performers. The Temptations were okay, but there was something about their attitude, it was totally different from ours. But then, I came to realize that the older guys – the

Four Tops were older too - were probably in the business just to have fun. They weren't in it to make money, because they already had a lot of money. They were just great, great people. I'd like to pay tribute to all of them.

Through the years, I was lucky enough to become acquainted with other singers who liked my voice and who tried to emulate some of the songs that I recorded. *That was quite a compliment*. For instance, Eddie Kendricks recorded "The Best of Strangers Now," the song that I did with the Fantastics. He recorded it on his first solo album. You can hear my version of it if you type in "The best of Strangers Now" by the Fantastics. And then, there are the many years that I had spent with the Chilites. On his first solo album, Eugene recorded a song that I had previously recorded, which is called "Puttin it Down to the Way I Feel About You Baby."

Along the way, I have met, worked with and enjoyed so many great friendships and experiences with thousands of wonderful people including: The Spinners, The Miracles, The Four Tops, The Chantels, The Cookies, The Three Degrees, Gladys Knight & The Pips, The Platters, The Drifters, The Temptations, The Four Seasons, The Commodores, The Impressions, The Jackson Five, The Manhattan Transfer, James Brown & The Famous Flames, The Chi-Lites, The Dramatics, The Delfonics, The Pointer Sisters, The Supremes, The Dells, The Five Keys, The Tavares, Sister Sledge, Chuck Willis, The Sensations, The Whispers, The Drifters, Jimmy Ruffin, George Clinton, The Parliaments, The Flirtations, The Flamingos, The Beach Boys, Dion and the Belmonts, Boyz II Men and Little Anthony & the

Imperials. I'm sure that there are many more to name but these are my earliest influences.

I could sit back now, especially when I play the old records, and remember all the great things that I've seen at work during that period. Entertaining has been such an awesome experience.

I had a great relationship with the Chi-Lites, to the point that they let their bass singer – TC Ramiro Anderson – take the place of our regular bass singer who was ill. They had decided to come over to England to do a tour and they brought Ramiro as a replacement. He knew he wasn't going to be a regular, but when he met me he said, "Hey listen, do you think you can find a job for me in England?" I told him, "You can join my group." So, by mutual agreement, the Chi-Lites allowed me to take TC from them and he stayed with me at my home in England. TC was in my first group of Realistics, and he was a tremendous bass singer.

TC became my son Blake's godfather. He had a bad heart, a really bad heart. He had a major operation in England and he had valves put in his heart, but still it didn't work and he died. He was in the group when we did the documentary from Belfast – it was Roy Bell, Stan, TC Anderson and myself – there were four of us then. That was before we became a trio because, once TC died, we couldn't replace him. Some of the Chi-Lites have died… Marshall and Duke are still living, but Eugene and Squirrel are dead. They were all wonderful people.

I also want to pay tribute to a group over here in England called the Spinners. Billy and the guys were great. They flew me over to Detroit to party with them, when they used to go on tours…it was fantastic. It's hard to believe that they are all dead now.

It's such a shame how life takes its toll, but the Chi-Lites and the Spinners were all very talented people and they are part of the history of music that we listen to all the time. Wonderful people.

The best part of my experience was having opportunity to perform with five of the best vocal groups in the World – Troubadours, The Velours, The Fantastics, The Realistics and The Magic Sound of the Platters, with some of the planet's greatest singers and musicians. I'll always remember fondly Brooklyn, New York where it all began and the guys that were there back in the day: Jerome Ramos, Donald Haywoode, Marvin Holland, Sammy Gardner, Kenneth Walker, Richard Pitts, Charles Moffitt, John Pearson, Troy Keys and Keith Williams.

JOHN CHEATDOM'S PHOTO JOURNEY

THE VELOURS - 1957
DONALD HAYWOODE
JEROME RAMOS
CHARLES MOFFETT
JOHN PEARSON
JOHN CHEATDOM
CALVIN McCLEAN

ONYX
45 RPM
45 RPM
Figure Music
(BMI)
512
CAN I COME OVER TONIGHT
THE VELOURS
Sammy Lowe Orch.

JEROME
RAMOS
DONALD
HAYWOODE
RICHARD
PITTS
JOHN
CHEATDOM

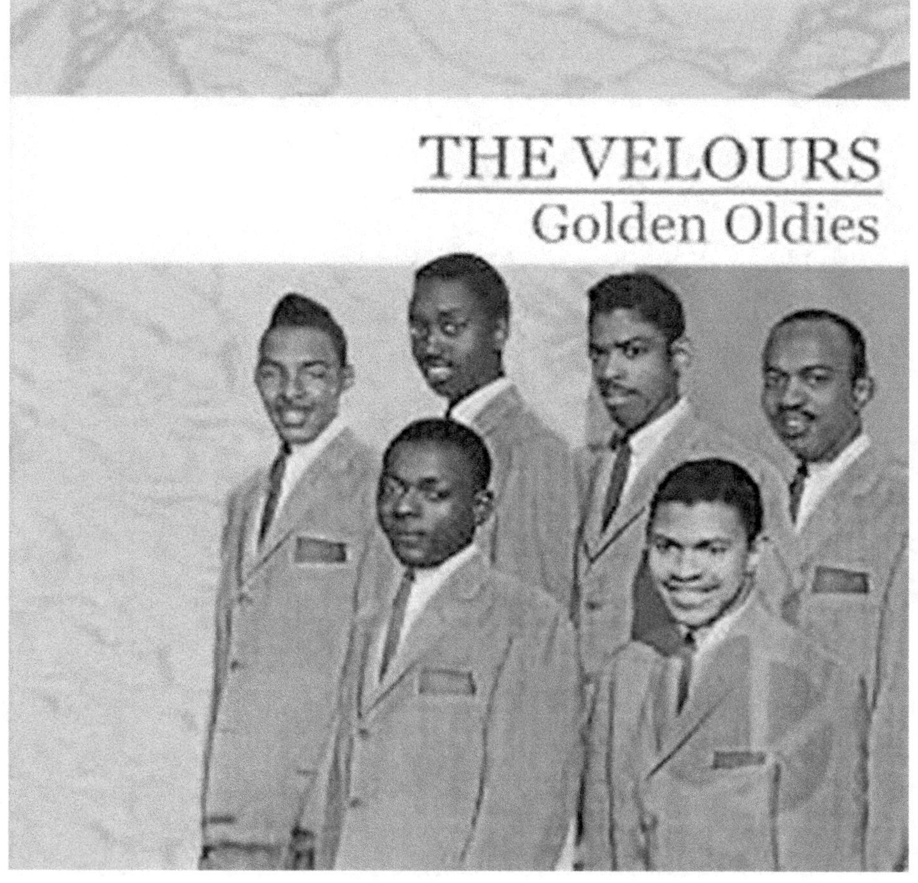
THE VELOURS
Golden Oldies

REMEMBER
WITH THE
VELOURS
ONYX

MAGIC
LET ME GO AND LIVE AGAIN

THE MAGIC PLATTERS

MAGIC SOUND OF THE PLATTERS
SIE LASSEN HITS WIE „ONLY YOU" & „HEAVEN AND EARTH" MAGISCH WIEDERAUFERSTEHEN

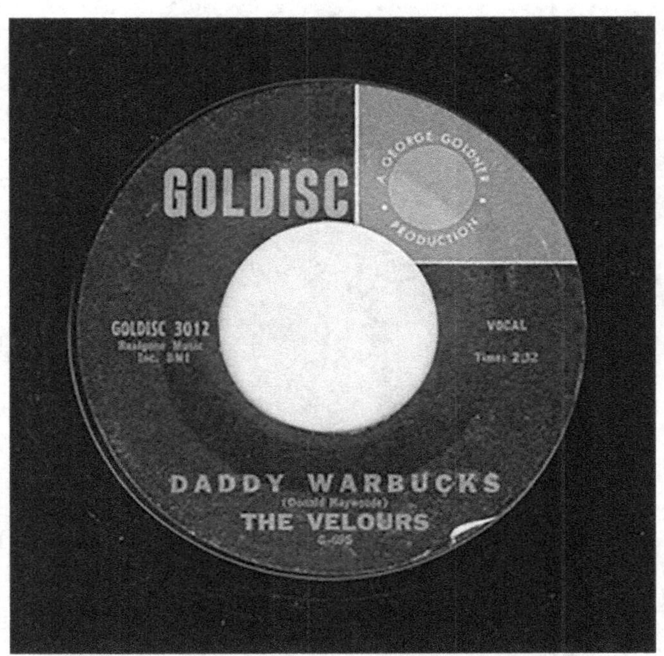
GOLDISC
A GEORGE GOLDNER PRODUCTION
GOLDISC 3012
VOCAL
DADDY WARBUCKS
THE VELOURS

ONYX
45 RPM
45 RPM
Figure Music (BMI)
520
REMEMBER
(Morrison-Crier-Winston)
THE VELOURS
Sammy Lowe Orch.
(5020 A)

45 RPM
END 1090
45 RPM
Under the personal supervision of
GEORGE GOLDNER
VOCAL
THE LONELY ONE
(Donald Haywoode)
THE VELOURS
G-771
A Product of End Music, Inc.
New York, N. Y.

CUB
45 R.P.M.
K9029
TIRED OF YOUR ROCK & ROLLIN'
THE VELOURS
CUB RECORDS—A PRODUCT OF LOEW'S INCORPORATED—Made in U.S.A.

bell
Cookaway Music
NCB
BLL 1141A 45
℗ 1971
BLL 1141
U.K. Recording
Prod. by
Macaulay/
Greenaway
for Mustard
Record Productions
SOMETHING OLD, SOMETHING NEW
(Macaulay—Greenaway—Cook)
THE FANTASTICS
Musical Direction by Gerry Shury

Here are the Fantastics, who debut on MGM with "Baby Make Your Own Sweet Music", an up-tempo swinger which was originally a big hit in the States for Jay and the Techniques. The boys are John Cheatdom, Jerome Ramos, Donald Haywoode and Richard Pitts, all born in New York and all educated at the same school. Jerome is actually possessor of the most esoteric degrees yet . . . he is a fully qualified, licensed embalmer. They've played around the ballrooms of Britain, with the British group the House of Orange, and have already built up a big following for their exciting visual performance

JOHN
CHEATDOM
JOHN
PEARSON
JEROME
RAMOS
AT THE APOLLO
DONALD
HAYWOODE

WATCH THIS NAME!

ONYX Records

(A New Label with "Old Hands" at its Head)

Current Release: "CASH BOX BEST BET"

The Velours

"MY LOVE COME BACK"

501

Released This Week:

The Joyettes

"STORY OF LOVE" | **"BOY NEXT DOOR"**

502

Watch for releases soon by these artists

The Pearls — The Marques — The Chordells

RECORDS, INC.

424 W. 49th St., New York 19, N. Y.

COlumbus 5-1872

LIVE
BROADCAST

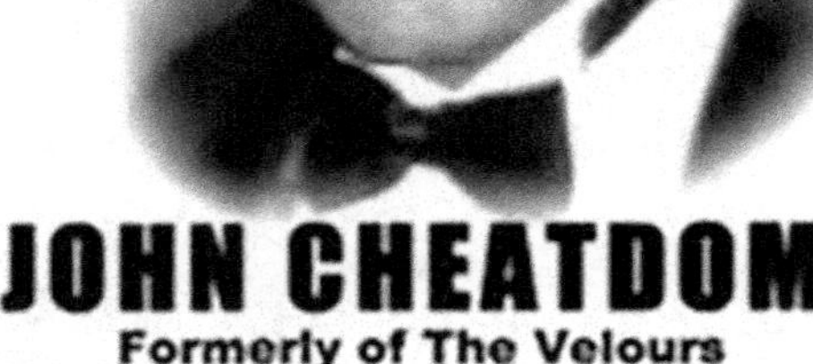

MAKING HISTORY
COME ALIVE ON...

JOHN CHEATDOM

Formerly of The Velours

RADIO!

EXPRESS

SATURDAY
OCTOBER 25

7PM(EDT) 6PM (CDT) 4PM (MST) 4PM (PST)
1PM (HAST) 12M (London) 11PM (EU)

www.blogtalkradio.com/clioexpress

★ A BILLBOARD SPOTLIGHT ★ A CASH BOX AWARD OF THE WEEK

BREAKING BIG IN BOTH POP AND R&B

"THIS COULD BE THE NIGHT"

"HANDS ACROSS THE TABLE"

ONYX 515

THE VELOURS

THE BILLBOARD SAYS

"Fine vocal by the lead with excellent group support on 'Night' makes the platter a hot contender in both pop and r&b markets. Medium-beat, rhythm backing helps create a listenable mood. The production on 'Hands,' the old standard, is similar and also appears a good bet to collect coin." (Oct. 21, 1957.)

THE CASH BOX SAYS

● The Velours come off their recent success, "Can I Come Over Tonight," with an even stronger wax, "This Could Be the Night." A slow beat tuneful ballad delivered with excellent teamwork. Romantic offering that has the qualities to take off. It has a beautiful melody with a couple of vocal gimmicks, a sincere reading and a story that appeals to the lovers. This should be the one to make the Velours a big box office attraction. The flip, "Hands Across the Table," is a strong reading of the lovely oldie. Good coupler, but we go all the way with "This Could Be the Night." (Oct. 26, 1957.)

ONYX RECORDS

424 West 49th St.
New York City. PL 7-5488

JUST THE FACTS

- Jerome Ramos and John Cheatdom, both previously sang in a high school choir called the Melody Men.
- The duo teamed up with Marvin Holland and Sammy Gardner to form another group called the Troubadours.
- The Troubadours then became the Velours.
- The Velours came to fruition during the mid-'50s, at the height of the Doo-Wop era.
- After being discovered at an Apollo Theatre amateur night, in 1956, the Velours signed to the Onyx label imprint.
- The Velours' first single, 'My Love Come Back' b/w 'Honey Drop' was released that year, but failed to chart.
- In 1957, The Velours released the ballad 'Can I Come Over Tonight' b/w 'Where There's A Will (There's A Way),' which was much more successful.
- The Velours released further singles in that decade, including 'Blue Velvet' b/w 'Tired of Your Rock & Rolling', 'This Could Be the Night' b/w 'Hands Across the Table,' 'Romeo,' 'Remember' b/w 'Can I Walk You Home,' and 'Crazy Love' b/w 'I'll Never Smile Again.'
- In 1957, Marvin Holland and Kenneth Walker left the group.

- They were replaced by Charles Moffitt and John Pearson (a baritone).
- Between 1958 up through 1961, The Velours switched labels to the Cub imprint.
- The Velours brought in Troy Keyes and Keith Williams (as a tenor), transforming the group into a sextet.
- The Velours released one album entitled 'Remember With the Velours".
- The Velours continued to record material up until 1961, after which the group went their separate ways.
- The Velours became the Fantastics, later in 1968, which continued to record and perform into the next decade.
- Remaining in England, John Cheatdom formed The Realistics in 1976. The group broke up in 1983, and Cheatdom then become part of a European version of The Platters, sometimes called the Magic Platters, who toured internationally.
- In the late 1970s, Charles Moffitt formed a new group, Charles Moffitt and His Velours. Charles Moffitt sang at United Group Harmony Association (UGHA) at times until he was murdered after returning home from a UGHA performance in 1986. His killer was never caught.
- The lead singer was Eulis Mason, the lead singer of Charles Moffitt's Velours continued the group name after Moffitt was shot dead. Charles Moffitt's Velours, featuring Eulis Mason, continued to perform and occasionally recorded into the 1990s.

- Jerome Ramos died of throat cancer on the 21st of October 2012 at the age of 75.
- Donald Haywoode passed away in August 9, 2015
- Richard Pitts is known throughout the UK, and other parts of the world have dubbed him as Mr. Fantastic. In the 50's Pitts sang with the Newtones and the Strangers out of Brooklyn, New York. In the 60's Pitts often worked at studio sessions with Gary Gant "a member of The Invitations" writing and Co-Producing together. Pitts eventually joined the Velours.
- Pitts is currently a music teacher at Huddersfield University in England.

ABOUT THE RECORD LABELS

Onyx Records

Onyx Records was founded in 1956 by record salesman Jerry Winston in Brooklyn, but the label rather quickly moved its offices to Manhattan, where for the next two years Winston drew largely on local talent to release an impressive series of vocal group sides, including: "Bohemian Daddy" by the Marquis, "Dearest One" by the Montereys, and "Can I Walk You Home" by the Velours. It was to be a short run for the label, though, with Winston folding it in 1958 and MGM Records picking up the masters. From New York, USA, the Velours - featuring the wonderfully expressive lead of Jerome Ramos, whose halting and vibrato-laden vocal style was one of the most intriguing in doo-wop - were one of the most impressive groups of the doo-wop era. Other members included Charles Moffett, John Pearson, Don Haywoode, John Cheatdom and pianist Calvin Hayes. The group first recorded for Baton, although nothing was released, but in 1957 they joined Onyx and success followed. Among their songs, 'Can I Come Over Tonight?', 'This Could Be the Night' and 'Romeo' were particularly impressive. The Velours also recorded "Can I Walk You Home" and "My Love Come Back" on Onyx - both with little success. The Velours broke up in the early 60s.

Deram Records

Deram Records was a subsidiary record label of Decca Records established in the United Kingdom in 1966. At this time U.K. Decca was a completely different company from the Decca label in the United States, which was then owned by MCA Inc. Deram recordings were also distributed in the U.S. through UK Decca's American branch, known as London Records. Deram was active until 1979, then continued as a reissue label. From the start, Decca placed pop records alongside progressive artists on Deram. Cat Stevens found early success there before moving to Island Records; and David Bowie's first album appeared on the label.

Bell Records

Bell Records was an American record label founded in 1952 in New York by Arthur Shimkin, A British branch was also established in 1967 and was active in the 1960s and 1970s. The Fantastics were among the first artists that recorded on the British label. Bell Records was reorganized in November 1974, which became the birth of Arista Records and the home of Whitney Houston, TLC, Barry Manilow, Tony Orlando and Dawn, David Cassidy, The Drifters, The 5th Dimension, Vicki Lawrence, and Melissa Manchester. The former catalogue of Bell Records and its related labels is now owned by Sony Music Entertainment (now a sister company of Columbia Pictures) and managed by Legacy Recordings.

DISCOGRAPHY

The Velours (members Jerome "Romeo" Ramos, John Cheatdom, Donald Heywood, Kenneth Walker and Marvin Holland)

Onyx 501 - My Love Come Back / Honey Drop – 1956

The Velours Sammy Lewis Orchestra (members Jerome "Romeo" Ramos, John Cheatdom, Donald Heywood, Kenneth Walker and Marvin Holland)

Onyx 508 - Romeo / What You Do To Me - 1957 (after this release Kenneth Walker and Marvin Holland leave group and are replaced by Charles Moffitt and John Pearson --- this is the most valuable of all their recordings)

The Velours (members Jerome "Romeo" Ramos, John Cheatdom, Donald Heywood, Kenneth Walker and Marvin Holland)

Onyx 512 - Can I Come Over Tonight / Where There's A Will (There's A Way) – 1957

Onyx 515 - This Could Be The Night / Hands Across The Table – 1957

Onyx 520 - Remember / Can I Walk You Home – 1958

Orbit 9001 - Remember / Can I Walk You Home – 1958

Cub 9014 - I'll Never Smile Again / Crazy Love - 1958 (on this release the group added another tenor - Troy Keyes (who in 1963 recorded on the Atco record label as a member of The High Keys and went on to make a number of solo recordings such as "Love Explosions" on ABC 11027 in 1967 plus a 1968 duet with Norma Jenkins "A Good Love Gone Bad" on ABC 11116). Troy Keyes sings lead on this release. Troy Keyes then leaves group and Keith Williams joins)

Cub 9029 - Blue Velvet* / Tired Of Your Rock And Rollin' - 1958 *originally recorded in 1955 by The Clovers on Atlantic 1052.

Studio 9902 - Little Sweetheart / I Promise – 1959

Gone 5092 - Can I Come Over Tonight / Where There's A Will – 1960

Goldisc 3012 - Sweet Sixteen / Daddy Warbucks – 1960

End 1090 - The Lonely One / Lover Come Back - 1961(after this release Charles Moffitt, Keith Williams and John Pearson leave group) -- John Pearson becoming road manager for The Flamingos ---- Richard Pitts formerly from The Newtones (who had a 1958 release on Baton 260 "Remember The Night") joins the group)

Relic 502 - Romeo / What You Do To Me – 1964

Relic 503 - My Love Come Back / Honeydrop – 1964

Relic 504 - Can I Come Over Tonight / Where There's A Will – 1964

Relic 516 - This Could Be The Night / Hands Across The Table – 1964

Rona 010 - Woman For Me / She's My Girl - 1966

The Velours (members Jerome "Romeo" Ramos, John Cheatdom, Donald Heywood and Richard Pitts)

MGM 13780 - I'm Gonna Change* / Don't Pity Me - 1967 *originally recorded by The Four Seasons as an LP track.

The Fantastics (in 1968 the group decided to change their name and take their chances as part of a Soul explosion in England. Members were Jerome "Romeo" Ramos, John Cheatdom, Donald Heywood and Richard Pitts)

MGM 1434 - Baby Make Your Own Sweet Music / Who Could Be Loving You – 1968

Deram 264 - Face To Face With Heartache / This Must Be My Rainy Day – 1969

Deram 283 - Ask The Lonely / Waiting Round For The Heartaches – 1970

Deram 334 - For The Old Times Sake / Exodus Main Theme – 1971

Deram 7528 - Face To Face With Heartache / This Must Be My Rainy Day – 1971

Bell 977 - Something Old, Something New / High And Dry – 1971

Bell 1141 - Something Old, Something New / High And Dry – 1971

Bell 1162 - Something Wonderful / Man Made The World – 1971

Bell 45,157 - (Love Me) Love The Life I Lead / Old Rags And Tatters – 1971

Polydor 2027004 - Baby Make Your Own Sweet Music / Who Could Be Loving You – 1971

Bell 45,279 – Best Of Strangers Now / Something To Remember You By - 1972

The Velours (members: Jerome "Romeo" Ramos, John Cheatdom, Donald Heywood, Kenneth Walker and Marvin Holland)
Lost-Nite 391 - My Love Come Back / Honey Drop - 1975
Lost-Nite 394 - Where There's A Will / Can I Come Over Tonight – 1976

Lost-Nite 400 - This Could Be the Night / Hands Across the Table – 1977

The Velours

Lost-Nite 402 - Romeo / What You Do To Me – 1976

Clifton 75 - C'est La Vie / Good Loving – 1978

Clifton 82 - Old Fashioned Christmas / I Wish You Love – 1978

The Velours / Buddy Knox

Roulette Gg-43 - Can I Come Over Tonight / Hula Love* - 1979 *flip by Buddy Knox. (Golden Goodies Series)

The Velours

Starlight 19 - This Could Be The Night / Mio Amore – 1984

Charles Moffitt & The Velours / James Myers Quintet

Clifton 100 - C'est La Vie / World of Fantasy* - 1985 *flip by James Myers Quintet.

Artists 136 - I Apologize / We Are Made as One - 1994 (1000 red vinyl copies made total - 100 were promo issue only)

ABOUT THE AUTHOR

JOHN CHEATDOM

...All in the name of music...

A TRUE UNSUNG HERO

John Cheatdom is one of the Greatest Falsetto Singers of his Generation.

Born in Brooklyn, New York, July 7, 1938 John is probably the only living singer who has had success as a lead vocalist in five different singing groups – The Troubadors, The Velours, The Fantastics, The Realistics and The Magic Platters. John has spent close to 70 years of his life performing throughout the world, in five different continents.

When John was sixteen years old, he began shaping his future while embarking upon a career as a professional singer in the entertainment industry. His music career began in 1953 when his group was originally formed as The Troubadours in the Bedford-Stuyvesant area of Brooklyn. The group later changed their name and exploded onto the music scene as the Velours, with the release of their hit record "Can I Come Over Tonight?"

At the age of 17, John was traveling all over America performing with the Velours. Their first tour was with all Black performers, and included: Ray Charles and his band, Mickey and Sylvia and The Moonglows.

Eventually the Velours broke up and John went to college, got a job, got married, started a family and stopped performing. After being presented with an opportunity to get back into show business, John reorganized the group and they went to London to work. Because of the instant success, John moved to London and relaunched his career as a member of what eventually became the Magical Platters.

At the age of 79, John continues to tour and has carved out a significant career and life for his family. He currently lives in London with his wife Rona and two sons, Blake and John.

ABOUT THE CO-AUTHOR

YVONNE ROSE

Yvonne Rose is the Co-Author of John Cheatdom's first published book, ***Keeping Doo-Wop Alive: One Man's Story of Strength, Stamina & Survival as an International Entertainer***.

In January 2001, Tony Rose, Publisher/CEO, Amber Communications Group, Inc. established Quality Press, a special service-book packaging imprint for authors who wanted to self-publish their books instead of waiting to gain an interest from mainstream publishers.

Yvonne Rose was appointed to head Quality Press and has turned over the last fifteen years many, many thousands of Self-Published Authors' manuscripts into completed books. As the Director of Quality Press, Yvonne and her professional team of editors, designers and printers, oversee the editing, design/layout, registration and manufacturing of every self-published author's books. She also consults with the authors regarding their marketing, production, promotional, distribution and publicity goals.

Some recently completed books packaged for self-publishers include: *I Need a Day to Pray* by **Tina Campbell (Mary Mary);** *Understanding and Negotiating 360 Ancillary Rights Deals-An Artist Guide To Negotiating 360 Deals* by **Kendall Minter. Esq.;** *Victory Together for Martin Luther King, Jr.: The Story of Dr. Warren H. Stewart, Sr., Governor Evan Mecham and the Historic Battle for a Martin Luther King, Jr. Holiday in Arizona* by **Pastor Warren Stewart***; Rising Up from the Blood: A Legacy Reclaimed-A Bridge Forward - The Autobiography Of Sarah Washington O'Neal Rush, The Great-Granddaughter of Booker T. Washington)* by **Sarah Washington O'Neal Rush;** *Poetry in Motion* by **Bill Raynor**; *How to Discover Real Truth* by **Leon Halfon**; *The Little Wire Hanger in the Closet* by **Hope Syndreamz**; *A Pillow of Comfort* by **Janice Richison**; *Nine Days in Italy* by **Warren Landrum**; *Nine Dresses* by **Renee Poignard**; and *The Black Buddhist* by **Meikle Paschal.**

Without hesitation, Yvonne is an unbiased motivator who takes the time to understand and address the needs of all first-time authors who want to do something positive with their lives – some have been on the wrong side of the law, some are recovering addicts, some have been abused, but all get the same respect and quality service. Yvonne is steadfast in her commitment to self-published authors who dare to dream big and feels that by introducing undiscovered literature to the world marketplace as bound books and eBooks, Quality Press can change the lives of millions of people in the United States and throughout the World. She firmly believes that "We are MANY VOICES sharing ONE EXPERIENCE…WE ALL HAVE A STORY

TO TELL, but only a chosen few of us are willing or able to share that story with the masses."

Because of Yvonne's beliefs and because of the company's thousands of satisfied clients, Quality Press has become the number one Self-Publishing - Book Packaging house for African Americans in the nation. Quality Press has a pool of top-quality editors and book designers with more than 200 years of combined experience in all genres of publishing and all facets of the media. The lineup of self-published books produced by Quality Press includes: non-fiction, fiction, biographies, poetry, business and career guides, children's books, cookbooks, urban, historic and romance novels.

Yvonne is a top requested author for public speaking appearances and an advisor to countless aspiring authors. She gives each author personal attention, answering all their questions regarding the rules and regulations and the ins and outs of the book publishing industry. Yvonne has received many accolades from her clients who come from all walks of life, including: doctors, attorneys, educators, coaches and lawmakers. *You're the best! Thanks for all your hard work! I love my book! Awesome job! You are such a motivating person. You inspire me!*

Yvonne has **ghost-written and co-written** several top selling non-fiction titles, including: ***Rising up from the Blood****: A Legacy Reclaimed—A Bridge Forward The Autobiography of Sarah Washington O'Neal Rush, The Great-Granddaughter of Booker T. Washington* (Solid Rock Books) by Sarah Washington O'Neal Rush; ***Natural Radiance****: A Guide for Ethnic Skin Care* (Global Skin

Solutions Publishing) by Pamela Springer; ***Fighting for Your Life:*** *The African American Criminal Justice Survival Guide* (Amber Books) by John Elmore, Esq.; ***Led by the Spirit:*** *A Sharecropper's Son Tells His Story of Love, Happiness, Success and Survival* (Strickland Books) by Robuster Strickland; ***Let Them Play****...The Story of the MGAA* (MGAA Books) by John David; ***A Journey that Matters****: Your Personal Living Legacy* (Lyceum Group Books) by Erline Belton; ***The Messman:*** *A World War II Hero Tells His Story of Survival and Segregation on the Battleship North Carolina* (Quality Books) by Yvonne Rose and John Seagraves; ***FREEZE:*** *Just Think* about It (More Than A Pro Books) by Levar Fisher; ***Seven Ways to Make the Grade***(Bob Lee Enterprises) by Doctor Bob Lee, WBLS Radio, New York City, Television host and Personality; ***Your Daily Dose of Quotes & Anecdotes: Featuring Words of Wisdom to Help You Make the Grade*** (Bob Lee Enterprises) by Doctor Bob Lee; ***The Biography of Charles Clemons Muhammad: A Man of Faith, Service and Community*** (First Choice Publishing) by Charles Clemons Muhammad; and ***Keeping DooWop Alive: One Man's Story of Strength, Stamina & Survival as an International Entertainer*** (Falsetto Press) by John Cheatdom.

Yvonne Rose is the **Associate Publisher and Senior Editor** at Amber Communications Group, Inc. Ms. Rose began her stint at Amber Books in 1998 as the co-author of the Company's flagship title, the national bestseller, ***Is Modeling for You? The Handbook and Guide for the Young Aspiring Black Model*** and has recently published, ***The Revised Second Edition "Is Modeling For You? The Handbook and Guide for the Young Aspiring African American Model*** (Amber

Books) and the International best-seller, ***Ageless Beauty: The Ultimate Skincare and Makeup Book for Women and Teens of Color***. (Amber Books)

For further information contact:

Yvonne Rose, Director, Quality Press

amberbks@aol.com

GRATITUDE:

I would like to pay tribute to the great guy's and doll's, I had the great pleasure of sharing the stage with over the years.

The Velours

Don Haywoode

Jerome Ramos

John Pearson

Keith Williams

Charles Moffit

Marvin Holland

Kenneth Walker

The Fantastics

Don Haywoode

Jerome Ramos

Richard Pitts

The Realistics

Jimmy Hamilton

Jimmy Cherry

Romaro "TC" Anderson

Sandy Sanders

The Magic Sound of the Platters

Ms Jackie Raas

Rowena Solomon

Maryline Blackburn

Patrice Murray

Ernest Wright

Kenny Seymour

Barry Smith

Tommy Smiley

Gee Bello

Dino Cassar

Wayne Topley

Milton Brown

Barry Ivan White

Charles McCaleb

Alan Cooper

The UK Drifters

Jay Washington

Rohan Delano

Luddy Samuels